CLAUDIO
RANIERI

PROUD MAN WALKING

CLAUDIO
RANIERI

PROUD MAN WALKING

CollinsWillow
An Imprint of HarperCollins*Publishers*

First published in 2004 by
CollinsWillow
an imprint of HarperCollins*Publishers*
London

© Claudio Ranieri 2004

1

A CIP catalogue record for this book is available
from the British Library

ISBN 0 00 719071 9

Set in Linotype Sabon by
Rowland Phototypesetting Ltd, Bury St Edmunds

Printed and bound in Great Britain by
Clays Ltd, St Ives plc

The HarperCollins website address is
www.harpercollins.co.uk

CONTENTS

A Special Note

Claudio Ranieri would like to thank Massimo Marianella
for helping him put his thoughts down into words.
Claudio will be donating all his earnings on this book to
Great Ormond Street Hospital for Children.

'I want you to go on managing the team'

I've always stood in front of the dugout during the match. It's been a habit now for many years; I couldn't even tell you how many. From that position I enjoyed the best possible view of the goal.

Gronkjaer had the ball wide on the right. With his trademark change of pace – in all honesty, something few others in the modern game are capable of – he cut in towards the middle, hit an inswinger with his left foot and found an incredible angle. Dudek couldn't get to the ball. Chelsea 2 Liverpool 1, and this after having been a goal down from Sami Hyypia's opener and then levelling through Marcel Desailly. We had stepped on the gas and overtaken our rivals in what was effectively a play-off, contested fortunately for us at Stamford Bridge. No small advantage this, coupled with the fact that of the three results possible on the day, either a win or a draw would have taken us into the Champions League.

Perhaps this is a little unusual for an Italian but I do not like playing percentages or speculating on the outcome of fixtures. This was never my way even as manager of Napoli and Fiorentina in Serie A, when we had to face the likes of Inter and Milan at the San Siro, or Juventus in Turin. I always prepare my team to win. I want to play for the highest stakes, every time. It was the same during my time as manager at Valencia, when playing away to Barcelona or Real Madrid, so it could hardly be otherwise in the Premiership.

This particular game on 11 May 2003 was one we all wanted to win. Why? Because there was something important on the line in terms of our future; because Liverpool had turned us over at Anfield in the last couple of seasons with performances that hardly justified the results; and because we wanted to show we were capable of achieving something together as a close-knit unit, with no help from anyone else, and without any possibility whatever of spending on the transfer market, especially as the state of the club's finances had been well known for a year or so following their exposure on all the front pages. In short, a mixture of pride and determination, competitive spirit and tactical skill was required. It was just the kind of situation I enjoy.

Running across the pitch and screaming, Jesper was celebrating a great goal. And we were all happy, because we knew it was a really important one, although at that particular moment, none of us realized just how important.

*   *   *

I loaded everything into the car. Alongside me was my wife Rosanna, and in the back, a few suitcases filled with summer clothes (and here's another myth that needs to be put to rest – the idea Italians and other Europeans have about the British summer. It really does exist, and can be as warm and enchanting as in Mediterranean countries). And there was 'Shark', my Alsatian, whose name was chosen by my daughter from the map of Australia in the atlas – perhaps it was Shark Bay that took her fancy – as a replacement for 'Boss', the name he had been christened with, and which could not work. There would have been too many of us around: me on the touchline, my wife, the dog . . .

On that trip back to London after a short break at the end of the season, I was carrying from Italy all my hopes and convictions for another season as manager of Chelsea. I knew I would not be able to ask for anything from the club in terms of buying new players, but knowing the squad I had got together, I was sure I could count on them to make certain we would enjoy our Champions League adventure and maybe even take a few important scalps during the season. After all, these would be the same players we had when we qualified for Europe in 2003, and the same who took us to the FA Cup Final in 2002. Frankly, as we approached Strasbourg on the motorway, I was wondering whether the club would be able to resist the temptation to sell Jimmy Floyd Hasselbaink and William Gallas, for the sake of the fans more than my own. I was aware that we had received good offers for both players and the money would help

3

to give the books a healthier look. Knowing the situation, I would not have objected, but they were two extremely important pieces in the Chelsea chess set. And what about Gianfranco Zola? Sadly, I knew I would be losing him, and through nobody's fault. I would have liked to have kept him on and so would the club, and he wanted nothing more than to sign and finish up his career with the No 25 shirt on his back, but it was obvious he would not be able to accept the only credible offer the club could possibly manage at that moment – a one-year contract with a cut in salary of 45%. This was never meant to be an insult in exchange for all the great things he had done for the Blues, not least the superb performances and 14 goals of this last season, but was intended rather as a heartfelt attempt to keep him. An offer made by a club that could not really afford the luxury. And so, I knew he would make the big decision: return home, play for Cagliari (his childhood dream) and, after so many years, be near his parents once again.

As I was thinking about all this, the mobile rang. It was Trevor Birch calling to tell me – at 11.30 pm – that Chelsea Football Club had been sold to a Russian business organization.

'What does this mean for us?' I asked. At that particular moment there were a thousand thoughts and a thousand images running through my mind, though in truth I was unable to picture any real scenario.

'No Claudio, don't worry,' he replied, 'from the little I've been able to find out about the new owner and the few words I've had with him, it seems clear he's someone who wants to achieve great things.'

Trevor's words sounded believable straight away, even if I could not yet form any impression of Mr Abramovich in my mind, much less of his enthusiasm and his potential to lead the club to better things. At any rate, I was reassured. Then, in a flash, a thought occurred.

'And Gianfranco?'

Suddenly I realized that the loss I assumed inevitable might still be retrieved.

'Is there anything we can do?'

I had spoken to him two days earlier and he had said then that the time had come to make up his mind. Massimo Cellino, the chairman of Cagliari, was pressing him and he could not put off the decision any longer; besides there were family matters to take care of, like moving house and schools for the children. So the next day he signed for Cagliari.

It was too late to change things. Although Gianfranco had not yet put pen to paper, he had given his word, and for him that was as good as a signature. About a month later, Cellino was a studio guest on 'Domenica Sportiva', a Sunday sports programme on RAI (the Italian state television), and I was speaking on a link from my country home in the Sienese hills of Tuscany. It was then that I learned all about the backstage activity that had accompanied Zola's signing. Cellino admitted that, having got wind of the extraordinary events happening at Stamford Bridge, he feared he could be in danger of losing

Zola even before he had landed him. For Cellino and for all Sardinia, this meant much more than simply acquiring a great player. Zola was a national symbol, a returning hero. He summoned Gianfranco to the club and proceeded to have all mobile phones and fax machines switched off. Once he had secured the player's signature, he admitted to the 'manoeuvres' and offered his apologies. Zola simply smiled, put his hand in his pocket and pulled out a fax he had just received from Chelsea, making him an offer hard to refuse. But, torn as he was between two great loves, he had already given his word. So yet again he had shown fantastic character, although it meant I was losing an exceptional person (quite apart from losing a footballer whose worth everyone knows). I probably never told him as much directly, but I was always genuinely proud to travel the world as Chelsea manager with a standard-bearer like Gianfranco. On the pitch, he enchanted and he scored sublime goals, but he was also our ambassador, our calling card, and an example on and off the field.

A few days layer, on 8 July, I was called into the office. I was to meet Mr Abramovich for the first time and I did not know what to expect. We met in the boardroom at Stamford Bridge. I went up alone in the lift but I was perfectly relaxed, even on this day that was going to change my life, although who could say in what direction? The Chelsea boardroom has no windows, but there is a certain light that emanates from the history in the pictures of the stadium that hang on the wall, showing how the place has evolved over the years. And we who wear the Chelsea jersey, in whatever capacity, are the ones who must keep the story going. It was precisely for this that we were meeting in that room.

Those present were Mr Abramovich with three close associates, me, and Trevor Birch. Instinctively, I spoke up first because I felt I had to make a clear statement concerning my own situation. I said that I had been around long enough in the world of football to realize that a change of ownership might mean a change in approach, or different objectives, and the direct consequence can be the decision to replace the coach. I would not have been upset; in fact I must admit I had already mentioned on the phone to a friend holidaying in Miami that, although I hoped otherwise, I sensed that my time as manager of Chelsea might even be over already.

'Tell me straight away,' I insisted, 'or else you risk wasting your time and money, and I could be wasting time as well.' Calmly and with the greatest sincerity, I had presented him with an opening, a perfect assist, to end my contract painlessly. No answer. Instead, he began to ask for my opinions on the team, and I saw immediately that he was fully informed as to how we were placed. For my part, I pointed out that even in our financial circumstances, we had already come a long way without buying players. What we had was an optimum basis for a team, but it needed strengthening. With the conversation now moving along more freely, he told me that he had seen the Champions League match between Manchester United and Real Madrid, and while watching it he had got to like the game of football so much that he had decided to buy a team. He admitted he had chosen Chelsea not because he was a supporter (at least not at the time, though he has since become a genuine fan, well beyond any level his business interests might warrant), but because when considering the list of clubs he could have purchased, ours presented the most favourable package. First and foremost, there was our history and the attraction of Champions League competition. I must confess, at this moment I suddenly thought about that goal of Gronkjaer's, a gratifying snapshot passing through my mind.

'What do you think this team needs to be able to step up a level?' he asked, perhaps simply to confirm what he was already thinking.

'Well,' I answered, 'considering that this is Chelsea and we have to contest the Premiership, the Champions League and two national Cup competitions, and try to win them all, I need two players to cover every position. If ambitions are going to be raised, we can't have a repeat of all the troubles we endured last year, when we started off brilliantly but then, what with injuries and bans, our prospects changed so drastically.'

I spoke on impulse, saying what I thought would be best for the club. He then looked at me, and stressed that he wanted to turn Chelsea into one of the top clubs in Europe – like Juventus, Real Madrid or AC Milan – adding also that he fully agreed with me on the need to have two top-class players for every position. At this point it was inevitable I would ask the question again.

'Tell me now,' I repeated, inviting a statement on the

coaching position, 'or you risk wasting your time and money, and I could be wasting my time too.' I was happy where I was and I wanted to finish the job, but in these situations, things needed to be made clear.

'No,' he said firmly, 'I want you to go on managing the team.'

For me, that simple declaration was enough. As of that moment it was possible to start working for the future. I told him I wanted young players who would show promise as future championship-winning material and who could also be mixed in with experienced players, because I wanted a Chelsea that would be capable of winning things right away, but also equipped to stay at the top level over time. The names I mentioned immediately afterwards also gave clear notice of another aspect I considered fundamental. Above all, I wanted players from the home nations capable of giving a heart, soul and spirit to the squad that would be essentially English in nature. I believed strongly in this. The backbone of a team should reflect the characteristics of the championship it plays in. Equally clear, and demonstrated by the arrival of Hernan Crespo, Adrian Mutu and Claude Makelele, was the importance of including star players from abroad – vital for making the step up in quality – but there should always be a strong local contingent, not least because the fans can identify with them more easily. After all, Manchester United and Alex Ferguson did this very same thing in the 1990s, though with a slight difference. What they did well was to bring up star performers through their own development structure – home-grown talent like Beckham, Scholes, Gary Neville, Giggs and Brown – and bring in players such as Kanchelskis, Stam, and, most recently, Van Nistelrooy from abroad to create a winning formula.

From that day onwards throughout the entire duration of the transfer window, I was in daily contact with Mr Abramovich by telephone, directly or through his associates, and the results were there for all to see. I have to say that we landed almost all the players we dreamed of signing. When making plans with an owner like this, everything is certainly much easier. It was a real novelty for me when considering all the chairmen I had worked under previously in Italy and Spain. While no less passionate, it must be said that none of these had shown the same readiness to back up my technical wishes with actions. Let's just say that in the past, the players taken from me and sold always outnumbered the players who were bought for me.

Having made our plans for the future at that first meeting and before the buying programme we discussed was so satisfactorily under way, I invited our new owner down to the training ground (a facility not exactly up to the standard befitting a club with a name like Chelsea) so that he could see it at first hand and get to know the group of players who were already preparing for the new season. I was very pleased when he took up the invitation immediately. When we arrived at Harlington, just a short distance from Heathrow Airport, I called the squad together on the pitch and presented all the players and members of my staff to Mr Abramovich, one by one. Beyond the exchange of a handshake and the usual pleasantries, I do not recall any of the players or staff saying or doing anything in particular – apart from Roberto Sassi, that is. Roberto is the little man you see taking the players through their warm-up routine on the pitch before every match, the one who prepares them meticulously every day in training. He has been with me since I was manager at Fiorentina, and in my book he is an outstanding professional, a great worker and a keen student of all the new fitness methods, whatever their origin. He became famous twenty years ago in Italy as the first to see the importance and exploit the possibilities of the computer in our work. At all events, Roberto is not only a friend, and for me an irreplaceable colleague, but also an incredible personality when you get to know him. Just consider the way he introduced himself on that day in July to Mr Abramovich.

'Pleased to meet you. I'm the second-best fitness coach in the world. The first is dead.'

His standing joke, of course, but remarkable that he came out with it in the presence of such an important new owner. And he has never told me who No 1 might be!

The first of the new players to sign contracts were the two goalkeepers Marco Ambrosio and Jurgen Macho, who had been bought with the limited finances available to the 'old' Chelsea, but were still quality players. They put pen to paper on 2 July, which coincidentally was not only the same day that John Terry signed a four-year extension to his contract, to my great delight, but also

11

the day that Ken Bates and Roman Abramovich formally completed the sale of the club and the share transaction with a handshake in the centre-circle of Stamford Bridge football pitch. Recorded for posterity by the photographers, that day changed the history of our club. And a few days later, the face of the squad also began to change, taking on the look I had in mind. The first actual deal under the new regime was made official on 10 July with the acquisition of full-back Glen Johnson. He and Wayne Bridge were two players I wanted desperately, because every time we had played West Ham and Southampton they had really impressed me. Both had given Jesper Gronkjaer a very difficult time and this had attracted my attention. A second point not to be forgotten is that both signings filled another requirement of primary importance to me: they were young and English. In short, they were the ideal first two pieces of the jigsaw that I, or rather we, had in mind.

Transfer negotiations took their course, and as the press threw out a new name every day on the front pages and the fans began to dream, we got on with our pre-season training, which we had decided to start on 2 July with the opening Champions League fixture less than six weeks away. The first few days were spent doing nothing more than exercising muscles in readiness for a more strenuous workout later. Right from the start of my coaching career, I have always combined fitness with work with the ball because I feel certain that the players will be more interested and more involved, and so they train better. This is an important stage of the season because you are storing up physical energy and laying the foundations for what is to come. This is all the more important in the Premiership, where the competitive side of things is absolutely fundamental. Many of my colleagues in Italy still keep faith with the ideology of exercise only at first, for a few days. My response is that you can do it all with a smile, simply by adding the ball. The programme for that first week, unlike the usual routine during the season, was based on two sessions with a break for lunch and a couple of hours' rest at the nearby Holiday Inn. Pre-season is a time that I particularly enjoy. Everyone is meeting up again after the summer, working together, talking about their holidays (perhaps telling one another about their successes with the fair sex – though not when I'm around!) and dreaming about what ambitions might be achieved in the year ahead. This year was a little bit different for Chelsea, with fresh topics being generated daily by the new direction the club was taking.

Unfortunately, it often happens that even before the first pre-season friendly someone in the squad will pick up an injury. On this occasion, the ill fortune suffered by our keeper Macho really was cruel. Not even a week had gone by since the Austrian had started training with us when, during the morning session, he was hurt while making a clearance. We realized immediately that the injury was serious, even before an MRI scan confirmed he had ruptured cruciate ligaments and torn a cartilage in his right knee. That evening I went home very upset because although no-one was to blame, it was a severe blow for the youngster, who would now also have to face an operation and thereafter a long period of rehabilitation. I had not lost a regular first-team player, because my first-choice goalkeeper was Carlo Cudicini, but in these cases it is distressing quite simply from a human point of view.

Having received the official news of Johnson's signing on 10 July, we set off the day after for Roccaporena in Umbria for the second part of our training camp. During my time with Cagliari and Fiorentina, I had regularly held training sessions there. The place was quiet and consequently restful, and not too hot, so that useful work could be done. No less important, the food was good, and this the lads appreciated. Here the group could really come together, in a place where individuals are a long way from London and therefore able to make friends more easily. The first time I went to Roccaporena it was practically a picnic site and nothing else. There was just one hotel with no television and only two telephone lines. Now things were very different. A local charity, the *Opera Pia di Santa Rita* (Roccaporena is very near the Sanctuary of St Rita of Cascia) had built and opened a new hotel with all modern conveniences. The food taken by the players was drawn up by the medical staff so as to ensure that whatever the players ate would be easily digestible and at the same time give them the nourishment they needed. For over a year now I had been Zone dieting, this involves sticking to a balanced intake of carbohydrates, proteins and fats, eating less but more often, which meant a few sacrifices. Fortunately the results have been good as I managed to lose 10kg or so, but when I was with the team I never ate anything different to them. It seemed to me only right and proper, since we were a team.

There was plenty of sweat and toil at Roccaporena, as this was the second week of training and the workloads were increased, but there were a lot of laughs too. The new arrivals had to go through their 'initiation ceremony', standing up on a chair and singing to the entire assembly during dinner. The proceedings were organized by John Terry and Frank Lampard, usually we would start throwing paper napkins, and finally everyone would clap. Traditionally, one of our massage team, Billy, would also stand up on a chair and entertain everyone, not by singing but by doing a bit of stand-up comedy. I must admit I didn't understand a word of it (it was only afterwards I found out I was not the only one) but I laughed fit to burst just the same at the way he told the jokes and the way he himself was laughing at the end. This was a wonderful bonding experience, which kept morale high and brought the squad together.

Obviously I do not get as physically tired as my players during the training camp, and so it generally happens that when they flop into bed exhausted (at least, I hope they do) I have a bit of time to myself. The usual phone call home, the usual scribbles in my notebook, jotting down plans and formations, and a chat with my staff, perhaps to find out how work is going with a specific player or more generally with the squad as a whole. All this and more, because after dinner, in the cool evening air, thoughts turn inevitably to what the coming season will, or at least might, hold in store. But this year had been different. There had been no time to think because, fortunately for us and thanks to the efforts of the club, the reality had materialized simultaneously with the dreams. I was in touch continuously with London, both in my mind and on the phone, as there was something important happening every day.

We had still not played our first friendly, a fixture against Lazio in Rome set for 18 July, when a second great piece of news arrived from Stamford Bridge. The Cameroon midfielder Geremi had been signed from Real Madrid for £7 million. I must say that I had had my eye on him for some years. In fact he could almost be considered a fixation of mine. I have always liked players who are tactically flexible, individuals with character who never give up and know how to defend. From what I had seen, before having him at my disposal on a daily basis, Geremi combined all of these qualities. It had been a blow to me when John Toshack, then the Real Madrid coach, plucked him from the Turkish club Glenclerbirligi, and I freely admit I had already asked Chelsea to sign him the year before. Now that the resources were finally available to acquire him, he was one of the names I had put on my list. He signed for Chelsea on 16 July, straight after Johnson and on the same day that Eidur Gudjohnsen also renewed for three more seasons. This was a pleasing coincidence for me, as it served to underscore what I had always thought and said. The squad that had taken us into the Champions League needed to be improved if it was going to aim for yet higher things, but not discarded.

Just a few hours later, before sitting down to lunch the next day, I received another important telephone call. I was told that the Blackburn winger Damien Duff had flown to London to begin serious talks with Chelsea and to undergo a medical. In reality the deal was not looking quite so much of a certainty the next day, as we prepared to play our first game of the season. Understandably, Duff had wanted a little time to consider his future carefully. The papers put out the news that Manchester United were stepping up their interest in him, and all we could do was wait for him to make up his mind, confident that we had offered him an attractive deal and the prospect of an equally exciting adventure at the highest level. Damien is a player with many qualities. Tenacious, fast, always ready to shoot, a good crosser of the ball. He was the classic footballer, with something extra. When up against Blackburn Rovers in the past, my main problem had always been to keep him in check, and I had greatly admired him during the World Cup in Japan and Korea – in this instance without the anguish of being on the opposing side – when for me he was the one who shone for the Republic of Ireland team. Damien is highly inventive, and in addition, although he prefers to play on the left, he has the great capacity of being effective in more than one position. From the opposite wing, for instance, he can cut in and shoot dangerously at goal left-footed, curling the ball much in the same way as Chris Waddle used to do back in the 1980s. And this was not all. Soon after having him in the side, I found that by playing him in the hole just behind the forwards, where he had never been used before, he could deliver assists of pinpoint accuracy to the strikers – just like the best playmakers in the NBA.

There's also a little secret I can reveal about Damien Duff. He is my mother Renata's favourite footballer. She is forever telling me so on the phone, and if this were not enough, she also said so when interviewed on Sky Italia. She described him as Chelsea's Nedved, and given that Juventus's Czech international won the European Footballer of the Year award this season, it seemed an auspicious comparison. It meant I'd have to think twice before I substituted him, otherwise she would have something to say! But even my mother, just like Duff and all my other players, must understand not only that every decision taken is strictly in the interest of the team – this goes without saying – but also that in such an important season we cannot afford to wear anyone down physically, because at the crucial moment, everyone must be at their best. They need to be ready both physically and mentally.

This was one of my concerns when we were drawing up our prestigious and well-stocked player roster. Everyone wants to play and always to have a great game. This is nice, and this is how it should be, but I am there simply to take the decisions that can help Chelsea lift as many trophies as possible. Sometimes the choices are not easy to make, but if there is one thing I have always done it is to shoulder my responsibilities, and I knew I would do the same this time around, except that every decision would attract more commotion.

Waking up on the morning of 18 July, I thought straight away it was probably no accident that the most important season of my career would be starting with a match, albeit a friendly, in my native Rome. It was neither an advantage nor a disadvantage, simply a question of fate. Thinking about it, all the big events in my life have had their beginnings within sight of the Dome of St Peter's. I was born in Rome, began my schooling there, and naturally my life in football began there too. I saw my first football match at the Stadio Olimpico, as a Roma supporter, and it was in that same stadium that I made my debut in Serie A, wearing the red and gold jersey. Now another important adventure was beginning for me, again in Rome, this time at the Stadio Flaminio, which is smaller than the Olimpico and decidedly seedier. It is attractive and has its own little history, but there is practically no football played there nowadays and it could do with rather more attention, although it has had something of a new lease of life in recent years since Italy began playing Six Nations rugby. The Flaminio also happens to be the sports ground nearest my current home in Rome, a nice apartment in the heart of the Parioli district, just a short walk away.

That game against Lazio was our first of the season, but precisely for this reason I was interested in just about everything bar the result. In any case this was not the real Chelsea, considering that of the new signings for the team we were building, only Johnson was playing and even he had only trained with us for two days. Nonetheless, the friendly in Rome confirmed to me that the eyes of the world were on our club, since as a result of the very fact that so much had been said about us, the stadium was full. Everyone had come to see puffed-up and ambitious Chelsea. We played as well as we could at that particular moment – in other words, not very well – and it was no surprise that we lost 2–0. Not that Lazio had outplayed us or shown themselves to be a stronger side, but they were at full strength and further ahead with their preparation, a factor which at this stage of the season makes all the difference in the world. We were still heavy-legged, whereas they were almost in top form and unquestionably brighter. Mr Abramovich was also in Rome to see the game, and I remember telling him not to be too concerned about what he had seen.

'Not to worry, Mr Chairman, I'm sure we'll come up against this side again in the Champions League, and then it will be a totally different story.'

I was ultimately proved right, though I would certainly not consider myself clairvoyant because of this. It was something I said, not in trying to justify the defeat, but because I genuinely felt it. I never like to lose, but in all honesty, even though it had happened in my home town and in our first match, I was neither disappointed nor annoyed. Certainly I was not worried, as I am old enough to be part of a generation that considered pre-season friendlies as a way of easing into competition, with no weight attached to the results. These attitudes have changed rather in recent years, with television involved. Now there is pressure to win everything, instantly, and it is no accident that early games are contested between teams qualified for the Champions League, rather than amateur sides. I knew this was only a first semi-competitive outing, and played without most of the team we would be putting together.

The next day it was back to London for a short break before taking part in a fairly important tournament in Malaysia. The Asia Cup was organized directly by the Football Association, with entry determined by final placings in the 2002/03 Premier League table. Four teams were involved: the Malaysian national side, ourselves, Newcastle and Birmingham.

We had problems with the trip back, as there was a strike on at Heathrow and so some time was lost before a flight could be found to take the party to Gatwick. Nothing too serious of course, but because we had only two days' rest I did feel a bit sorry for the players who were going home – I would be flying out straight from Rome – although I have to admit my mind was on other things, and above all on the transfer market. Duff had still not signed and the rumours linking him to Old Trafford continued to make the headlines, but I knew about the commitment and determination of our new owner, and when I happened to notice a girl leafing through one such paper at the airport, I had to smile.

Taking off at noon on Monday 21 July, we honestly did not know that this particular day would be potentially one of the most important in the club's history.

If not the most important, then certainly the most expensive. As we slipped across the skies on our way to Malaysia, two more players signed contracts with us: Wayne Bridge in the morning, and Damien Duff in the afternoon. A total cost of £24 million to the club, and a great double present for me and all the fans.

The flight lasted twelve hours and when we arrived in Kuala Lumpur at 7 am local time, aside from the good news, we were all a bit weary. Time for Professor Sassi to take charge of things. Tiredness and the need to get the body moving have to be balanced against the temptation to give in to jet lag and flake out on a bed. The lads did some stretching and a few exercises in the hotel, so that we at least avoided going straight out into the heat. I had taken my family along, certainly not with any intention of belittling the tournament, but because I felt that visiting the Far East would be a nice experience for them. Ultimately, no-one was disappointed because it was a genuinely constructive trip, from all points of view. The members of the squad began to get to know each other better, it was in Malaysia that the work done previously began to be put into practice, and while we were getting on with our job, my wife Rosanna and my daughter Claudia also enjoyed themselves, as I expected. I too was satisfied with the outcome, for all of the technical reasons mentioned, though in all honesty I never like going to such far-off places during the pre-season period. I worry about the effect of long hours in flight on the players' legs and, especially in this particular case, the impact of a climate where the heat makes proper recovery impossible. I was afraid we might start off badly and that it could then have taken us more than a month to get back into optimum condition. We could not avoid the heat, as in any case it was sweaty even standing still, but on the other hand Sassi as usual had done his homework very carefully and we organized ourselves accordingly. We did a lot of stretching, and when training on the pitch we worked a great deal on ball possession.

It was also a pleasant experience from a social perspective, because all the teams stayed in the same hotel and this was a nice way for players and staff to meet, spend time and eat together; in other words, a chance even for opponents to enjoy each other's company.

After a delay of twenty-four hours, Duff and Bridge also joined the party, accompanied by club doctor Neale Fraser who had completed their medicals. The jigsaw was not finished yet, but it was beginning to take shape.

That Wednesday there was also a highly enjoyable official reception with a banquet at the British High Commission, given in honour of the three teams, who naturally were present. The next day was a match day, but before the early training session (8.30 am was the only time of day to beat the climate), we received the news that we had been drawn in Geneva to face the winners of the clash between Maccabi Tel Aviv and Zilina in our qualifying round of the Champions League competition. Decidedly not the kind of tie one would have asked from a benevolent Hand of Fortune, but we did not pay too much attention. In the evening we were due to play, and we did so in front of 20,000 enthusiastic spectators.

As the highest placed of the three Premier League teams at the end of the last season, our first match in the tournament was against the Malaysian national team, and on paper it should have been easy. Looking at the scoreline afterwards, there had in effect been a difference between the sides, although we had to sweat to make the final – in the true sense of the word! The heat was stifling and the opposition, being used to it, were extremely quick on their feet. We went ahead through Forssell after 35 minutes and they equalized four minutes later. Then in the second half we stretched away with goals by Hasselbaink, Gudjohnsen and Johnson. In addition to the goals and the win, I made a record in my notebook of two assists by Duff.

The next day was Saturday and I left the players free to do as they pleased, not as reward for a victory that might have been taken for granted and which clearly had no great significance, but because recharging the batteries is always very important. As for me, I took the opportunity to dedicate some time to Rosanna and Claudia. I don't want to sound precious and in any case I am simply not the type, but obviously they are the most important part of my life and to have them there made me very happy. And their presence perhaps forced me to take a break mentally, as I needed to, otherwise I know I would have spent my time on more plans, deals and ideas for next season. Taking the mind off the job at that moment would be good for me as well. We went to see the Butterfly Park and the Bird Park, which were beautiful and relaxing. Then when the time came for lunch we sought out a typical Malaysian restaurant. In London, which is a wonderful city from this point of view and with so much to offer, Rosanna and I try out every kind of cuisine possible and imaginable (Claudia lives mostly in Rome where she is studying Political Sciences at university). So what better occasion to enjoy a good meal than this? Fortunately we did the rounds of the market after eating, because on one of the stalls we saw something – my daughter and I didn't have the courage to ask what animal it might be – that looked rather like a chopped up rat.

A little shopping next, and for my daughter this is very rare, but to round off the day we went to try a Thai massage. The best place, they told us, was in a hotel situated on the other side of a lake from our own. Getting out of the boat, we also walked across a golf course, which at sunset was a truly enchanting spectacle even for me, although (don't hold it against me) I never play the game at all. Once they had shown us into the special rooms we were curious to see how it was all done, and with what kind of ceremony, who we might meet . . . European managers? Local politicians? Then the doors opened wide and who did we find? Of course! Some of my very own players, including the inseparable Bridge and Johnson who, quite rightly I must say, had had the same idea as us. It was both an experience and a way to relax.

On Sunday, with news arriving from London that the negotiations with Manchester United to bring Seba Veron to Stamford Bridge that had started a while back were still deadlocked, we took the field for the final. This time there were nearly 42,000 spectators on the terraces, and what is more, we had Newcastle as our opponents. In this match we definitely played well, even if the score remained 0–0 after 90 minutes. And there was a good performance from Alexis Nicolas, who had a start in this game. The young Cypriot midfielder regularly captains our reserve side trained by Mick McGiven, a man of great importance to our club. To decide the destination of the trophy we had to go to penalties, and at 3–2 we really thought we had it won, because next up was Jimmy, and he had never missed from the spot for us. But their keeper Given surpassed himself by diverting the ball onto the post, and after Bellamy then scored it was down to sudden death. John Terry (JT) put away his kick and at that point it was the turn of Jermaine Jenas. He tried to chip the keeper, but incredibly sent the ball right over the bar. Instinctively I looked at Bobby Robson, realizing in the same instant that we had won our first trophy. He was furious, and still fuming in the dressing room, so I believe. Terry was captain and it was he who lifted the Cup, which I trusted would not be the last of the season. It was also my first trophy with Chelsea, and, hoping it would be the first of a big collection, back in the dressing room I picked up JT's jersey, which had the Asia Cup emblem blazoned on the arm (like the Premiership emblem on our regular jerseys). I got John to autograph it subsequently at Stamford Bridge. And so we left Malaysia decidedly wealthier in practical experience and memories, and with one indelible image – our fitness coach, Roberto

Sassi, naked on the table in the middle of the dressing room (a good thing he's small . . .) dancing with the Cup tight in his grasp. One thing I could be sure of: I already had the makings of my squad.

AUGUST

'The squad has changed . . . rotation is going to be a fact of life'

Back in London and immediately there was the media to face. The first of August was the day of our presentation press conference. Everyone sun-tanned and looking relaxed, this was always an enjoyable time, although this year there was so much to talk about. The presentations alone took up an enormous amount of time, almost two hours, and, as I expected, the attendance was massive. There was no Macho unfortunately, due to his injury, but all the other new signings were present: Geremi, Johnson, Bridge, Duff and Ambrosio. This was a day, I would say, when we had definite confirmation that our squad would be the cover story of the season. No pressure as far as I was concerned, simply an exciting situation.

To be honest, the nice part was that the presentation was a foretaste of more to come, though at the time there was no certainty about the next move. Well actually, I did have an idea or two . . .

In fact, there would be another red-letter day just four days later. Two new purchases. And not just any two players, but Seba Veron from Manchester United and Joe Cole from West Ham. And in one shot! Brilliant. Really and truly, a manager could hardly ask more of a club. For most of my counterparts in the league, even one from a possible two would be a dream, let alone getting both. On the other hand, a club with big ambitions needs high-quality players, and these two were at the very top of my list. The great thing was that Chelsea had managed to keep me happy, bearing in mind the value of the players and their importance to our plans. First it had been Bridge and Duff, and now another brace of top players had arrived at Stamford Bridge on the very same day.

Joe Cole is an investment for the future, but he will be useful in the present too. He really is a natural talent like few others, and has a Latin streak, with his unpredictability and imagination. But this is not all. In my opinion he has incredible potential for improvement. He needs to develop a little self-control, precisely because he is so eager, always wanting to dribble, using up too much energy in the middle of the park. He can and must learn to do all this in the final third of the pitch, where such skill can be deadly. For the good of the team and especially for his own, I hope to be able to contribute to his improvement as he gains experience by playing. He could be an important factor in my plans to open up opposition defences on days – and who can say why, but even now I sensed there could be quite a few – when we happen to find them packed tight.

As for Veron, obviously there is nothing I want to teach him. He is already one of the world's best midfielders, in my opinion. He failed to hit top form at Manchester United for a number of reasons, but with us I feel sure it will be a very different story. I will certainly be looking to exploit his desire for the chance to shine again. The desire all great players have. And then again, I am used to working with Argentinian players, having coached Gabriel Batistuta at Fiorentina and Claudio Lopez at Valencia, to name just two.

If encouraged and given free rein to show his class, Seba can change the face of our team. The thing I liked immediately, in addition to everything I already knew about him, was his personal approach. When we spoke for the first time after his contract had been signed, he showed a tactical flexibility and an appetite for work that will help us make great strides, I feel sure.

Having got over our jet lag, training was again fully underway and we were ready to resume our schedule of pre-season friendlies, fortunately all in and around the London area this time, so we would avoid the burden of travelling. I cannot really speak for my English colleagues, but where pre-season games are concerned, I certainly hold with the Italian school of thought. Friendlies are simply the best way of measuring workloads. Our usual practice is to work especially hard on the pre-season training camp, and the first few matches then serve to put the players under a little extra competitive stress. That is the usefulness of these games, rather than the results themselves.

The first was against Crystal Palace, at Selhurst Park, where we quickly went 1–0 up through Mikael Forssell, who really does continue to fulfil his promise. He has a remarkable strike rate, obviously a factor to keep strongly in consideration, along with the unqualified admiration I have for him. He has a goal-scoring instinct typical of the great strikers, and I know he has a great future in store. Mika is a fighter on the pitch, but he has the right attitude in training too. It has happened more than once that I have had to get him out of the gym or off the pitch, for fear of him overdoing his training. He always has the right outlook, and this I like. Clearly, he will need time to make a full recovery after the serious knee injury that has sidelined him for almost a year, and for his own good this means plenty of games – something we cannot guarantee here at Stamford Bridge, particularly given the number of star forwards in the squad. In the interests of everyone concerned, we need to find him somewhere to play. He has admirers in several leagues – in Serie A, in La Liga in Spain and above all in the Bundesliga where he has already played on two occasions – but I would prefer him to go and play in a Premiership side so we can keep a close eye on him and measure his progress against our own standards.

We ended up winning the game against Palace 2–1, thanks to a Geremi free-kick at the end of the first half. For me this was nothing new, but with the trajectory he conjured up to beat the wall, many eyes were probably opened to the abilities of this young man, not least his shooting power. Perhaps a friendly against Crystal Palace on their own ground was not the ideal place for Geremi's prowess at free-kicks to emerge, but now we all knew that this was one more weapon we could count on.

If anything surprised me at all, it was the number of people who had come out on a hot August afternoon to watch a friendly. There were over twenty thousand spectators in the stands. On the other hand, there were two factors at work here: the huge support given by Chelsea supporters anywhere and everywhere, which I was already familiar with, and the interest in our team shown by football fans generally, which I was coming to appreciate.

Three days later, and we had another friendly at Watford. Another win, and in terms of the scoreline an even more convincing one since we put four past them: Forssell, Hasselbaink, an own goal, and, finally, Duff. The boys were understandably a little tired after the work we had been doing, having trained twice the day before, morning and afternoon, but generally speaking their physical condition was very good, and the squad was taking shape as I wanted – indeed as we had all hoped, me and my staff, and the management. One particularly important aspect of the game against Watford was that we had Manu Petit back too, after the operation he underwent during the summer. Here is a player few can match for character, and for his influence on the field. He has won so much in his career, always leading from the front, and I know that if he stays fit, if I make the best use of him physically and psychologically, he can make a difference to this team. He only came on for 20 minutes to replace Lampard, but it was a significant return nonetheless.

For me and for the team, all this was a stimulus to be converted into success. For the press, it was a pressure situation. Pressure? Pressure is what I had at the start of my career with Campania Puteolana, when there was not enough money to pay wages, and unsavoury-looking types would be seen hovering around the ground. Pressure is something the Italian press know how to generate, when thirty or so journalists from newspapers, radio, commercial and network TV turn up at the training ground every day. When the fans are heavily opposed to what you are doing. When you are expected to get results while your club chairman is selling players instead of buying them. All this is pressure, but there is no pressure in having a team full of medal winners at your disposal and a chairman like Roman Abramovich who (on the basis of everything that had happened so far, obviously) always had a positive attitude and continued to bring in fabulous players. In any event, I knew well enough that a good start was needed, especially if we were to avoid idle rumours springing up from outside. And a good start meant doing well in our first two away games: the Champions League qualifying round, and the opening Premiership fixture at Anfield.

We knew our objectives, the difficulties we would face in pursuing them, and how we intended to go about things. We knew all our Premiership opponents. What we did not know yet was who we would be facing in our first Champions League fixture. So, because I prefer to leave nothing – but nothing – to chance, the next day I went over to Budapest to watch the match between Zilina and Maccabi Tel Aviv. The Israelis had more to their game, but allowed their opponents too much space. The Slovaks were better organized and quick on the counterattack. The fixture was being played at a neutral venue and this probably helped Zilina, who in securing a draw were the surprise winners of the tie. So now we knew who our opponents would be. For my part, and with all due respect, I had seen enough to know that if we avoided doing anything silly we would go through to the group stages. This was the same day that the signings of Joe Cole and Seba Veron were announced. Could I sleep more easily now?

More training, and then I was off on another trip. That Saturday, Liverpool were entertaining Valencia, and for me this was an occasion not to be missed. The excuse – a perfect one – was to take a look at the Reds, who we would be playing the week afterwards in the first fixture of the new Premiership season. In reality I was killing two birds with one stone, as they say, since it was also a chance to see my former club Valencia again. Ah yes, the best wish I can make for myself is that when looking back some day, the memories of my time in London will be as happy as those of the time spent at the Mestalla Stadium. The Valencia job was something that happened almost by chance, when I rather set off into the unknown to replace Jorge Valdano, who had been sacked (and who now, of course, is general manager at Real Madrid and one of the most influential men in football). It turned out to be one of the most wonderful experiences of my career, and of my life. The club, but more especially the people of Valencia, captured my heart. Life can be magically unpredictable and irrational, but for whatever reason, they took to me straight away (and perhaps it was fate that led me to return to them). True enough, we won only a Spanish Cup while I was there for my first spell, but for a footballing town that had won nothing for so long, it was a significant success. I initiated the policy of loaning young players out to pick up experience in the lower divisions, just as I ended up doing at Chelsea. I did this, for example, with youngsters like Albelda, Gerard and Curro Torres, who were to return a few years later as key components of the subsequent La Liga-winning side. They appreciated at Valencia that I had laid the foundations for a new era at the club, and I have always regretted not having stayed longer the first time to reap what I had sown. I left because of a misunderstanding with the club. I had the feeling that Valencia did not want to invest in the squad. To win a La Liga title, two or three more players were needed to make the step up in quality, and at that particular time the club could not spend.

And so I found myself going to Atletico Madrid. This was a difficult experience as Atletico had hit a sticky patch at the time, but there were absolutely no regrets as I enjoyed working with the colourful and eccentric Jesus Gil and his family, even if I never finished the job I went there to do. As far as Valencia is concerned, perhaps in a certain sense I was happy to have been wrong, because they went on to some great achievements, winning a La Liga title and a Spanish Super Cup, and have appeared in no less than two Champions League finals, and as a supporter of theirs I was delighted. I am sure there are many in Valencia who support Chelsea too.

I was able to meet up again at the Liverpool game with, among others, Dr Jorge Candel, who is not only one of the best doctors I have ever come across in my career but also a wonderful person, and with Amedeo Carboni, a player who should be an example for any professional to follow. He's nearing 40 now, but has always been one of the best defenders in the game and is absolutely indispensable. Not only on the field but, as the saying goes, for his influence in the dressing room as well. Off the pitch, he is surrounded by marvellous women – no lie, this, because besides having a special partner in his wife Giacinta, he can also boast four adorable daughters!

Valencia won the match against Liverpool 2–0, and I was happy for a number of reasons. Among other things, I received a splendid piece of news the same day. We had completed our purchase of Adrian Mutu from Parma. Maybe Adrian was not particularly well known in England at the time, but in Italy people were well aware of his worth. In my eyes, he was just the man we needed: a forward, though without being an out-and-out striker. I was looking for a fast and tough player who would never stand still; a player with superior ability to score goals, but equally, one who knows how to deliver the final pass. He had all these qualities, what we in Italy call a 'second striker'. He had just had a good year with Parma, for whom he also scored plenty of goals, but now we were offering him the chance to make a big leap in quality with us. We paid a lot for him, almost £16 million, but I know he was also worth a lot. A thought occurred to me on the way back to London. We were in Italy when Glen Johnson was signed. I was on a flight to Malaysia when they told me that the negotiations with Duff and Bridge had been concluded. I was in Budapest to watch the Zilina game when Veron and Cole were brought in, and now here I was at Liverpool when the Mutu signing was agreed. And remembering that I had received a call in France, on my way from Rome to London, telling me that Chelsea Football Club had been bought by Abramovich, I can only come to the conclusion that I ought to travel much more in this life!

My little joke, of course. These must just be coincidences.

In my mind, I was already thinking about the formation I would put out against Liverpool the following Saturday, though without realizing that in the case of Mutu, who in the line-up of my thoughts would be one of the starting eleven, it was going to be a race against the clock from that moment on. Everything was squared with the British authorities in three days, and a work permit secured. At the Italian end, things were a little more complicated on the transfer front. Problems with faxes, a public holiday in mid-August (can it really be true that we Italians are always on holiday?), red tape . . .

anyway, it was not long before I realized I would probably not be picking Mutu to play at Anfield.

Before Liverpool though, we had to start thinking seriously about Europe, because at last, after all the transfers, the friendlies, the fine words and the expectations, this was the start of the real business.

We set off very early on the Tuesday morning. Rendezvous at Harlington 7.10 am, then on to Gatwick to take a flight for Slovakia at 11 am. Two hours' flying time followed by a coach ride of nearly three hours, and we were at Zilina. Arriving at five in the afternoon, we were soon on the field for the customary final pre-match training session. We found the temperature quite pleasant. Hot, but not suffocating. The match was the important thing, but no less important to me was the general attitude of the squad. For the first time here, I would be sending star players to sit out the game up in the stands, and it was only right that I should make things clear. Since I had brought everyone along with me, and this was our official debut, it was the best time. And so, I gathered all the players together the evening before the match to say a few words, especially to the older campaigners, as I had already spoken plainly to the newcomers before they signed.

To build a team, matches must be lived to the full. Not only wins, but defeats too, as these help to shape the character of the squad. In the end, a team is like a family and the hard moments should serve to bring everyone together. A defeat provides an important moment in which to take stock, and a base on which to build the wins that will come later. I wanted them to reflect on this as well, before we went into the first real competitive fixture of our season.

'Boys,' I said, 'one way or another, on the park or on the bench, you all knew where you were. But now you'll have to take on board the fact that it all starts from scratch. You've got to get used to the idea of having another manager.

'Imagine this is Eriksson speaking, or another international team manager. Then it won't be too difficult for you. What would you do? Try and put yourself about a bit so as to get noticed? I don't want you to show me anything I already know about. What you're worth, I mean. But remember that when I put you on the bench or in the stand – *and it's something that will happen to all of you* – it doesn't mean you're out of favour.

'The squad has changed just as the aims of the club have changed, and rotation is going to be a fact of life. Bear in mind that if you're here, new or old, it's because I want you along, so we can accomplish something big. If you all understand this, it will be the first step on the road to achieving the targets we've set ourselves.'

I had given them straight talking and I knew they had all understood, and that they all appreciated the situation. And I knew they would all pull faces when left out. Unfortunate . . . but they would simply have to get used to a new reality. Football has moved into a new era, and anyone who fails to grasp the situation will not have a great future. This is the time to lay foundations for a big structure, and there can be no question of those foundations being shaky.

MSK Zilina v Chelsea, Champions League Qualifier, 1st Leg,
Pod Dubnom, 13 August 2003

I decided to play 4–4–2, but in particular, to start Veron on the right. Zilina took the field adopting a cautious approach, with a lone striker up front and little appetite for attack. They were obviously wary of us even with home advantage, more so than against Maccabi, their opponents in the previous round, but hoped to repeat the upset by exploiting space on the break. As it turned out, they had one chance at the beginning, when after just three minutes Desailly was forced to make a rather scrambled clearance, but after that little or nothing else. We played the match as we should have, deservedly running out as 2–0 winners with a goal by Eidur Gudjhonsen and an own goal also resulting from a move of his. Getting off on the right foot is always important, and even more so for us, with all the talk that Chelsea generated during the summer. But besides the result, I was happy about the attitude of the squad and the tactical flexibility I had sensed.

The Liverpool date was already near, but the transfer window had not yet closed and I was hoping not only that the players I had asked for would materialize, but also that they would be available as soon as possible, with preparation of the squad in mind. The bigger the names, the more complicated the negotiations turn out. In discussions with the management we had agreed to look for a holding midfielder and a forward. However, they had to be players who could make a difference to our squad, and, given the top-class players we already had, the circle was now closing on possible targets. For the midfielder, I was very keen on Claude Makelele, not least in view of the fact that he was unsettled at Real Madrid; and for the forward, I liked the look of Hernan Crespo, or, alternatively, Fernando Morientes. Inter wanted to sell the Argentinian as they needed cash, but they were asking too much, whereas in the case of the Frenchman at Real the situation was more complex, diplomatically in particular. My plan, as I had explained clearly to Abramovich right from our first meeting, was to cover every position with two players, both of whom I could consider as first choices. I needed another two pieces for the jigsaw, just like these.

In the meantime, the great day had arrived. No Mutu unfortunately, since, as I had feared, the transfer documentation from the Italian Football Federation did not come through in time, and we were at the airport ready to board for Liverpool. Ready for the biggest and most exciting adventure of our career. The 2003/04 Premiership campaign was about to get underway.

Liverpool v Chelsea, Anfield, 17 August 2003

We were taking up more or less where we had left off at the end of last season. A token of continuity that produced a positive feeling inside, though needless to say, Jesper Gronkjaer had scored that famous goal at Stamford Bridge three months ago, whereas now at Liverpool we were about to embark on a new era. It was a match like any other against top-level opposition, and simplicity itself to prepare for from the psychological standpoint. It practically prepares itself. The wait is exciting for everybody. Everyone is on edge, and in fact my job sometimes is to lower the tension. The problem was, I would be missing not only Mutu, but the injured Petit as well.

So I decided – keeping faith with my nickname 'the Tinkerman' – that I would field a completely new line-up. Yes, even though this was such an important match, I had no doubts about my decision to pick what I saw as the side that would give us the best result. I was putting the maturity of my team to the test, straight away. On paper it was a 4–1–4–1. In practice, I had Geremi in front of the back four, Johnson, Terry, Desailly and Bridge, then two central playmakers in Lampard and Veron, a lone striker up front, Gudjhonsen, and two out wide ready to cut in from the wings, Duff on the right and Gronkjaer on the left. An odd sort of formation in the eyes of the press, but I saw it as giving them both the chance to get themselves into shooting positions on their preferred foot.

Houllier had his usual 4–4–2 with Owen up front and Heskey and Kewell (wonderful footballer) playing off him on either side, plus the threat of Murphy able to score or provide from further back. They were playing a diamond midfield, frequently changing the point man to upset our plans.

A good game and at the end a great result, though it was certainly not easy. In recent years we had always

43

been undone at Anfield and punished well beyond what we deserved, and this time we all wanted it to finish differently to ensure a good start to our new adventure.

Liverpool started strongly, with Carlo saving well in the first few minutes from Murphy and coming out to deny Owen, but after that, everyone began to discover the new Chelsea: a team with the right balance, attitude, character and top players. Qualities summed up in our first goal, scored appropriately enough by Veron who, with perfect timing, finished off a splendid build-up involving Johnson, Desailly and Lampard, with the final surge and cross coming from Gronkjaer.

Perhaps it was the importance of an eagerly awaited match, or the names of the players and teams involved, but it hardly seemed like a season opener. High tempo, a lively atmosphere, the feeling of something already being at stake. I had made my three substitutions, introducing Gallas, Cole and Hasselbaink without changing the plan, and we seemed to be controlling the game without too much trouble. Then a mistake. Bridge was surprised by Kewell on the left-hand edge of the area, and knocked him over. Whistle. Penalty. The way the match was going, a draw would have been an injustice, and when I saw Owen send his spot-kick wide I was thinking almost that we had earned the mistake. But hardly had the thought occurred when, incredibly, the referee ordered the kick to be retaken because Carlo had moved. He judged that the half-step forward made by Carlo to launch his dive was illegal. Absurd! Unfair both in a sporting sense and from the standpoint of the rules as well, because on this basis every penalty awarded would have to be retaken or repeated ad infinitum. There was nothing I could do, but I was furious inside. I must have said something to the fourth official, though I cannot really remember what. And to think I am sometimes accused of being impassive, hiding my feelings! Frankly this was too much, but all I could do was watch as Owen converted. Back to square one, and in my mind I was already battling the demons of the last two encounters we had played and lost at Anfield. Legendary temple of football it might be, but precisely for this reason I did not want it to become a permanent jinx for us.

But then, three minutes from time, Jimmy latched on perfectly to one of Lampard's splendid passes and scored, releasing all of our anger (and his too, I imagine, as he had started the game on the bench). Off came the shirt, and as he paraded his muscles, he was symbolically showing off the muscle of the entire team. Yes, we really had carried on from where we left off, with a win against Liverpool. But in different conditions. Different players and different perspectives, but the same aim: to be a team with big ambitions. In this sense we had just passed a test of no mean importance, athletically and mentally, and I was obviously very happy.

Hardly any time to celebrate, though, and I soon had other situations to address. We had still not wrapped up the negotiations for Makelele and Crespo, but I was optimistic for a successful outcome on both deals.

Unfortunately, having top-class players also means having to do without them when their national teams are playing, and indeed after the win at Liverpool I had to witness what I knew all too well would happen. Harlington was almost deserted, with nearly all the likely candidates being called up either to the Under-21s or to the senior international squads. This is an impossible situation and there is no solution. We simply have to make the best of it, hoping that no-one gets hurt, although injuries are not the only risk. There are long journeys, jet lag, and above all it is practically impossible to plan any kind of physical training that will be the same for everybody. Sassi does his excellent best on the fitness side, but he certainly cannot work miracles. I never complain, because this is a problem common to many of my counterparts. And in any case, if you want to coach a top-flight team it is inevitable.

The following Wednesday, Carlton Cole accepted the idea of going on loan to another Premiership club. I was keen to secure this kind of arrangement for the same reasons as applied to Forssell, except that instead of going to Southampton as we originally thought, there was no need for him even to move house, as he went to Charlton. I know the surroundings are good over there. Alan Curbishley is a first-rate manager and there is also Paolo Di Canio, who can teach a young player plenty, most of all in terms of professional attitude and love for the game. Paolo possesses an in-born talent and has a big personality, but commendable passion too. Carlton needs to mature, but if with his extraordinary potential he can learn from Paolo, he will come back to be an important player for our club.

I had wanted to travel up to Ipswich to see the England–Croatia game, but instead I decided to go to Upton Park where Carlton Cole and Glen Johnson were playing in the Under-21s. Unfortunately, the result was a resounding 3–0 defeat for David Platt's team. I met up with Sven-Goran Eriksson in the VIP stand and exchanged a few words in Spanish with Sammy Lee, a Liverpool legend and one of the England coaches, who I imagine must have picked up the language in his playing days at Osasuna. It was a pleasant chat with Sven – and who knows what the press would make of that! But this was the least of my worries.

Chelsea v Leicester, Stamford Bridge, 23 August 2003

The first home game of the season had arrived. Always an important occasion. There are positive vibes in the air that give the team a special boost. This year of course, the importance of everything is double or even greater. The team was introduced to the strains of *Kalinka*, that best-known of all Russian songs, and it seemed to me an engaging, clever, almost ironic way to present the official opening of a new page in the history of the club at Stamford Bridge. It has since become an enter-taining ritual. I am always in the dressing room with the team when the announcements are made, but I see from television recordings that Roman Abramovich enjoys the idea too, undemonstrative as he is, standing up and clapping in time with the music.

On the pitch though, it is our job to dictate the tempo,

and despite the setback of having Geremi sent off for a second yellow card, we picked up the three points against Leicester too. A foregone conclusion perhaps, but only on paper. We played 4–4–2 because being at home, naturally, I wanted a more attacking line-up right from the start, with Mutu and Hasselbaink up front. I knew it would not be the goal-fest some might have expected, because our opponents had nothing to lose and they would defend any way they could, so at the end I was pleased on two counts: the result, and the fact that Mutu had scored a great goal on his debut. He struck a free-kick right-footed from about 25 yards, and when the rebound came back off the wall, proceeded to despatch the ball into the net with his left. In the space of a minute, to people in England who knew nothing about him, he showed himself to be a winner, a player with an eye for goal capable of shooting accurately and powerfully with both feet. He was eager to make an impression and I was pleased he managed to do just that.

A couple of days later, one of the two pending transfer deals was nicely wrapped up at last. Crespo was now a Chelsea player, and even if the financial commitment was considerable at £17 million, the news was certainly something to celebrate. Hernan has lots of experience although he is still relatively young. Above all, he is a player with 109 goals to his name in Serie A, effectively a harder league for a striker than most others, which means he comes with a solid pedigree. He's a clever foot-baller, the classic opportunist in the penalty area, with fine anticipation and good in the air. In short, he's the complete forward. I tell you, a manager will always do a few sums before the start of a season. He tries to assess how many goals are likely to come from individual players, or rather from the various field positions. Say, 5 or 6 from defenders, at least 10 if not 15 from midfielders, and then a good haul from the forwards. So, if I had done my forecast again on the day Crespo arrived, I would easily be thinking in terms of another twenty or so coming from the Argentinian. The hope will be that he can justify our confidence in him by scoring them.

Chelsea v M&K Zilina, Champions League Qualifier, 2nd Leg, Stamford Bridge, 26 August 2003

On the same day the Crespo transfer was confirmed, we played the return leg of our Champions League tie with Zilina. With a 2–0 result from the away leg and the superiority over the opposition that the scoreline suggested, this honestly was the comfort zone, but I was by no means going to make wholesale changes simply in the name of squad rotation, not wanting to send any wrong messages to the team. I gave Joe Cole a start and reintroduced Celestine Babayaro. Nothing sensational. I also brought on Robert Huth in the second half, and the German showed straight away that he was worth his place on the pitch. A nice headed goal and a free-kick that hit the post proved to me there were points to mark on his card. All plus. Armed with a genuinely dangerous long-range shot, he is also good in the air and has fine defensive qualities. Okay, these are things I had already seen from him in training and friendlies, but to have them confirmed in an official fixture, and a Champions League tie at that, was better still. Typically German, he has character and a strong physique. I am sure he will have a future in the team even if, like Forssell, it may be best if he goes out on loan somewhere next season. With his goal and two more from Johnson and Hasselbaink, we managed to win 3–0 and I was delighted, since we had achieved our main short-term objective of making it to the Champions League group stage. If anything, I was a little surprised by our opponents, in a negative sense; they came apparently looking to defend at all costs, even after having lost their home tie. I found this inexplicable. After the first-leg defeat, their chances of qualifying had perhaps already gone, but they could have at least used this occasion to put in a good performance. Instead they lost, and their refusal to play football contributed nothing to the show.

Two days later, the draw for the group stage was made in Monte Carlo. I watched it live on television, sitting on the couch at home before lunch, and it did not spoil my appetite in the least. I work on the principle that all teams are tough until you play them, although I must admit that some of the groups looked trickier than ours, at least on paper. We drew Lazio, Besiktas and Sparta Prague. True, it could have been much worse, but equally the widespread optimism I sensed on the day seemed to me to be premature on the one hand, and dangerous on the other. I guessed the mobile would start ringing because there would be journalists wanting to get my first impressions, but I suspect they were getting the busy tone, what with all the relatives and friends who were already organizing themselves for the double-header with Lazio. I recalled what I had said to Abramovich in the dressing room at the Flaminio after our defeat there in the friendly. My intuition had been right. Now we had to add the result. Still, I could not help marvelling at my own magical powers of prediction . . . and no black wizard's hat!

Chelsea v Blackburn, Stamford Bridge, 30 August 2003

We closed out the month with another home fixture, this time against Blackburn. A game I was wary of, because they are a solid side, and at the time we were to play them I was thinking that they were in for an excellent season. They have good players, an expert and strong-willed coach, and a big enthusiasm that runs right through the organization. Blackburn are the club where Damien Duff came to maturity, in every sense, and naturally I had plenty of questions to face about him during the Friday press conference at Harlington. This gave me the chance to reiterate how I see him, in my plans, as a fundamentally important piece on the Chelsea chessboard.

We had barely kicked off when Desailly made an elementary mistake on the touchline, uncharacteristic for a player of his stature. So it was that after just 19 seconds we were already chasing a goal by that man Andy Cole. If

51

this were not enough to convince me of the way things were going, on the half-hour we had a Mutu goal disallowed. And although I never like to criticize the referee and his assistants, it looked good to me. But Mutu stepped up again soon after, swerving around Brad Friedel after good work by Hasselbaink and Veron and netting the equalizer. A great goal at a really critical moment. In the meantime I had made a change in midfield, as I soon realized that Veron would be struggling out wide on the left. I put Geremi on the right, Lampard in the middle, Duff on the left and brought Seba into the middle too, but further forward. In practice, he was now playing just behind the strikers. One minute into the second half, and Cudicini delighted everybody by spectacularly tipping over a David Thompson drive from around 25 yards out, but then misjudged the ensuing corner and unwittingly allowed the visitors to take the advantage again through Cole. From where I stood, I was unable to see exactly whether or not Petit, jumping in front of him, had touched the ball (I saw later on the TV that he did not actually get a touch) but no matter. The important thing at that moment was to equalize, not worry about mistakes. And even if Carlo had got it wrong coming off his line in that particular situation, too bad. It happens, and these are the moments when we all do better to remember how many times a goalkeeper has claimed the ball successfully. I had put Petit on to replace Duff so I could deploy a midfield diamond with the right balance. Manu in front of the defence, Veron behind the strikers, Geremi on the left and Frank on the right.

I know Duff would have liked to stay on against his old club right to the end, but I had to take what I thought was the best decisions for the team, and at that stage, this was the best solution as I saw it. Ten minutes later we had our equalizer, a penalty converted by Hasselbaink, and even if this was the first time in the campaign we had not won, in the end I was satisfied. I have seen enough football to know that when things start to go wrong as they did right from the kick-off of that game, salvaging a point qualifies as a success.

Another remarkable day to mention before turning the page of the calendar. Right at the last minute, before the transfer window was due to close, the final piece fell into place. Claude Makelele. A player remarkable for his ability as a ball winner and an organizer in defence, and special for his experience of wearing the jersey of a winning side like Real Madrid. Really and truly, I could not be more convinced of this buy. If Real have been at the top in recent years and dominated in Spain and Europe, between the defence and the halfway line they owe it to this man. Of course it is the players like Zidane, Raul, Figo and Ronaldo who make the headlines, but the trophies have come no less by virtue of Makelele's efforts. To have his winner's mentality and competitiveness at the heart of my midfield made me breathe more easily. The jigsaw was now complete and for this I could only thank the club and praise the enthusiasm of Roman Abramovich. I had searched out all the components that could link up with the others. Not just tactically but in view of whatever I could learn about each one, directly or indirectly, even with regard to their character. Assembling a team with so many new players takes time. No-one was going to give us too much of that commodity, I knew, but at that point I was also aware that the core of the squad was made up of high-class players, and this should reassure us. I say 'us' because everyone would be under pressure and at the same time eager to succeed in a great undertaking.

At least two covering each position. All first-choice players. All medal winners. Now we were on the right track. It would be up to us to show that this was the squad to deliver the goods to our chairman, who had made it all possible, and to our fans whose affection for the team deserved to be repaid.

I liked to change my formations, because I knew I had players with the tactical flexibility to be able to do it, but listing them for the sake of convenience as a conventional 4–4–2 below, for the season to date, creates an impressive picture. What's more, it's a pleasant dose of responsibility.

I repeat, if everyone can see that they are all indistinguishably indispensable to the success of a common purpose, then we really might achieve the great aims set for ourselves. All the elements are in place, but I also know very well that it can be difficult for a player to accept the decisions of the coach, even though we are all professionals. Maybe there will be a few long faces now and again, but I still feel that, content or otherwise, everyone will know my decisions are taken in good faith. I am confident that our relationships will be frank and

	Cudicini		
	Sullivan		
	Macho		
	Ambrosio		

| Johnson | Terry | Desailly | Bridge |
| Melchiot | Gallas | Huth | Babayaro |

Gronkjaer	Lampard	Veron	Duff
Geremi	Makelele	Petit	Cole
Stanic			

| Mutu | Crespo |
| Hasselbaink | Gudjohnsen |

open, and I would like to have the same confidence, even at this early stage of the season, that we will be putting new silverware in the cabinet.

SEPTEMBER

'The first thing they ask me is why I didn't play Bridge. Is this a joke?'

Taking a good look at the calendar during the summer, it was the month of September that appeared the most complicated, even if – or perhaps precisely because – it is the month with the fewest fixtures. September, of course, sees the start of the Champions League group stage and the long break from club football when internationals are played.

Perhaps one day in my career I will be offered the chance to coach a national team, and to be honest, in another ten years or so I would quite like to do it. Then I will see the problem from the other point of view, but from where I stand at the moment, these breaks are a burden on the club. Of course the needs of the national teams cannot be ignored, but it is a heavy imposition to have my players going off in numbers to all parts of the globe at this critical time. Certainly, if you want world-class footballers in your side then you know beforehand what to expect, because obviously they all represent their countries, but even knowing this, it is a situation fraught with difficulties. Especially in this instance, because of how quickly it comes around, after only a few Premiership fixtures. You start and then stop again, and this is not good for any kind of group endeavour. It is the same for all clubs, but because Chelsea have so many new players and we need more than other teams to find the right mix, it is worse for us. Being together at this stage is fundamentally important for team spirit, familiarization with plans, physical training, relationships in the dressing room . . . But there is no way around it, and all a manager can do is concentrate on the players he still has. There may not be many, and none are too fortunate either, since their efforts and attitude come under even closer scrutiny.

I gathered together the players available to me at our semi-deserted Harlington ground and, with the help of my staff, took the opportunity to put them through a few basics – physical mainly, but technical too, why not? It is actually rather an odd sensation seeing the dressing rooms half empty, and though it is nice to be able to park the car without a major struggle, there are problems with the organization of training matches too. To make up the numbers, I asked Mick McGiven (our invaluable reserve-team coach) to bring a few youngsters along, so that they could get the chance to test themselves at a higher level, and I had the opportunity to see them at close quarters. Whenever commitments with the first team allow, I always go along to see youth- or reserve-team games, and not only because it is a part of my 'duties'. I love the Chelsea jersey whatever the level of the player who wears it, and quite apart from the professional obligation involved in hearing the day-to-day reports that Mick and youth coach Steve Clarke pass on in our dressing room, and finding out if there are one or two youngsters who have been making good progress. Steve Clarke was a defender in his playing days, a Chelsea stalwart from the 1997 FA Cup-winning side. In addition to his coaching duries he would often scout for me, and provide written reports on opponents.

I enjoy simply standing on the terraces and cheering. There is the risk sometimes in these games at Harlington that the younger ones may get pumped up and overdo things a little. Fortunately no-one has ever been overcompetitive to the point of hurting a first-team player, which can happen in football from time to time. Some years ago in Rome, just to give an example, Paul Gascoigne was dealt a serious injury by a very young Alessandro Nesta – who went on to become one of the best central defenders in the world.

It was also a month that opened with an important announcement regarding the history of the club. At the season's first meeting of the Chairman's Supper Club, Ken Bates stated officially that he would be stepping down in 2005 to become Life President. It is certainly not my place to remind Blues supporters of how important Ken has been to Chelsea, as his name will always be written large in the history of the club, but I would just like to include a word or two about our personal relationship. It's a surprisingly 'beautiful friendship', in a certain sense. Surprising, because it is confined almost exclusively to the time spent in flights to and from away games. I rarely go into the office, he never visits the dressing rooms, and so our meetings are in reality somewhat sporadic. Something must have clicked between us – who knows what? – because I'm sure he has fondness for me just as I feel affection for him. I was amazed when, still with a year and a half left on my contract, he wanted me to sign up for another five years with the club. This was a huge offer, not least considering the current economic situation in professional football in general, and at the club in particular. It was a decision that made me extremely proud too, because it was a gesture made by someone who can be seen always to have acted wisely in the interests of the club. Prior to the renewal, I had worked with commitment, and extremely hard. I had taken the club to an FA Cup Final, though we had still not laid our hands on a trophy. So in all sincerity, what had persuaded him to offer me this important extension? I think he must have appreciated the way I work, and the way I am. He understood that I was taking on the job enthusiastically, even though it was a difficult time for the club. Bates was the right man in charge during an extremely complex period in the history of the club. Thanks to his foresight, his total devotion to the cause and his courageous decisions – unpopular sometimes, but necessary – Chelsea FC have been able to keep the respect due to a club in the very top flight of the game. He made sure a collapse was avoided in the 1980s and opened the door to a new era that promises to be even more exciting and, I hope, full of success under the new owner, Roman Abramovich.

Chelsea v Tottenham, Stamford Bridge, 13 September 2003

We had had to wait a couple of weeks for the resumption of the Premiership, but finding our concentration and the right level of determination was no problem at all, with Tottenham waiting for us. In fact, I soon learned from the fans during my first year in London that of the various derbies played in the course of a season, the biggest for the Blues is the one against Spurs. The atmosphere is awesome even to me, and I have been involved in some big local derbies too, in Rome as a player, and in Madrid as a coach. The great thing for us 'non-English' is to see how the fans can display passion, fervour and pride for their teams without it spilling over into violence. I know there was a problem during the 1970s and part of the 1980s, but now it has all but disappeared. As an Italian it is something I can only admire, and even envy in some measure, as things are very different back home. Obviously I do not want to point the finger at anyone in Italy, but really one has to applaud the police and the clubs for the work that they have done in this country, and the civilized behaviour of fans everywhere. It was so good to see supporters mingling outside and inside the stadium with their different coloured shirts and scarves, knowing that many of them travelled on the Underground and walked together from Fulham

Broadway station with no quarrels and no problems.

The occasion was extraordinary not only for the atmosphere created by the supporters, but also for the brilliant sun shining down on London, ready to light up this big, big derby. We started off with a classic 4–4–2, with Petit in midfield and Mutu and Jimmy up front. I was especially happy at being able to give Manu a start for the first time after a long injury spell. For me, he is a world champion in the true sense of the word: unbelievable determination and leadership, and footballing skills that everyone has admired down the years. At the beginning of the season, when we sat down with Abramovich and the new management to discuss the individual players we already had in the squad, I explained at length just how important Petit was to our cause. A player who has the ability to be decisive in so many ways on the field, and whose return, even in a side full of medal winners, was of absolutely fundamental importance. To see him in the middle of the park in the biggest derby of the season was hugely satisfying for all of us.

After twenty minutes or so Tottenham went 1–0 up – Frederic Kanouté the scorer – and I decided straight away to change things around, playing three at the back with Melchiot alongside Terry and Desailly. I needed to restore the balance tactically. I knew even beforehand that with Hoddle normally playing a back line of three and a playmaker (Jamie Redknapp in this instance) between the defenders and the midfield, we might run into difficulty, but this is precisely the reason I often make changes during the course of a game. First I want to see if my team can adapt to situations as they arise on the pitch, then, if necessary, I make adjustments. It is a way of helping my players to develop, to show their tactical maturity, but obviously, getting the result must come first. Having found the right setup, and with the determination we had, I felt sure we could win the game. And indeed after just a few minutes we equalized, thanks to a nice collective effort rounded off with a header by Lampard from Gronkjaer's cross. A few seconds later and we were ahead, Mutu scoring from an assist provided by the ever-dependable Duff. This is how a great team responds: forceful, showing character and determination but staying clear-headed. Another moment of significance for the season came in the second half, when I decided to bring on Makelele. He had been on the bench at the start, as I wanted him to get a good look at his new surroundings before taking part. Claude was the last player we had bought, but certainly not the least in terms of importance. He would be the balancing element in midfield. I have always believed that top teams should have a key midfielder playing deep. Besides being quick, Claude had the knack of always being on hand to help out his fellow players, and positioning himself in the right place at the right time. So, could I have picked a better match than the Chelsea–Tottenham derby to introduce him to the atmosphere of the English game?

Still echoing in our ears was the cry of 'Muuuuu-tuuuuu . . .' that always goes up when Adrian scores. Running onto a brilliant through ball from Joe Cole, he made the result completely safe. It ended 4–2, and this was a very important game in several ways. It was a good performance following the break, albeit with minimal preparation; the debut of Makelele; the ability to come from behind; the win; and some nice goals and assists.

There had been a few concerns certainly. These were early days with the new look Chelsea, but the players seemed to be putting themselves under pressure needlessly. It was irritating that we only seemed to get into our stride after going behind, and that having worked to put things right and opened up a two-goal lead, we then allowed our opponents to pull one back. The boys had to work on their concentration, and I said as much at the post-match press conference. But it was a win, and with three points in the bag I was not about to start losing sleep over things I knew we could put right.

It was good to have the memory of the derby win to take with us into that other big adventure we were about to embark on: the Champions League, now more than ever the competition everyone dreams of winning. Myself included, naturally. As a player I never even came close, but as a coach I knew that the European stage was the one of the best places to 'discover' a player or see particular game plans being put into practice.

Sparta Prague v Chelsea, Champions League, Group G,
Toyota Arena, 16 September 2003

The calendar had us making our Champions League debut not only in a wonderful city, Prague, but also against a particularly well-balanced team, Sparta. The first surprise I had on the trip was when I walked into my hotel room. They had given me an incredible suite. I had never seen anything like it before in my career, and probably never will again. It had four en suite bathrooms and even a billiards table! I doubted whether I'd even have time to explore it all in the two days we were there, but it was so big we could have trained in there with the entire team.

Playing in the Champions League is not exactly the same as playing in international competitions, however good these may be. It was for this reason I decided to leave Duff and Lampard on the bench initially. I wanted to avoid loading them with too much responsibility, and instead chose a starting line-up with players who already had this kind of international experience. It was a decision I had no regrets about, regardless of the way the match turned out, though I was persuaded by what happened on the field to put both players on at the beginning of the second half. We started with a diamond midfield: Makelele in his usual position, Petit on the left, Geremi on the right and Veron behind the two strikers. Sparta were looking almost exclusively to defend, and we had to try and open up the game and create chances for ourselves. As it transpired we created many in the first half, but Mutu and Crespo – whom I had selected precisely on the basis of their previous experience – were unable to capitalize. With the introduction of Damien and Frank I changed the entire formation completely, pulling the diamond back into a line across midfield and bringing Veron deeper behind Crespo to give him more space. In the end we deserved to win with a goal by Gallas and it was an important strike, because getting off on the right foot is crucial in this type of competition, especially away from home. Scoring goals is not such a rare occurrence for Willie, and in fact he had won a bet the year before among the French members of the team (Petit and Desailly being the others) as to which one of them would score the most goals by the end of the season. He is good in attack because he is always ready to exploit even the slightest advantage in dead-ball situations. It was very nice to start off our Champions League campaign with a victory, and I like these wins that come late in the game. Wins secured with a struggle are the best. They show the team is battling right to the end to get the result it wants. And it was nice to share the success with the more than 1,200 Chelsea fans who made the trip to the Czech Republic. Addressing the post-match press conference, I quipped, 'Well, I'm still in my job, contrary to what some people in the press are predicting. Maybe I should sack myself and do them a favour.' Controversial statements are generally not my style and the delivery was light-hearted, not least because I genuinely had no reason to doubt the soundness of my relationship with the new management. On the other hand, with all the dreary negative comments that contrasted with the results, I had felt obliged to make a point in some way.

Back in London, we needed to look after a few players who had picked up injuries on the trip: Mutu and Desailly had ankle problems, Veron was complaining of a troublesome Achilles. Nothing too serious, fortunately, with an away game at Wolverhampton next up.

Before going up to the Midlands, the club made an announcement that would be highly significant for the future of Chelsea. Paul Smith, advisor and trusted associate of Peter Kenyon, was appointed as consultant to the board of directors. This was obviously to fill in the statutory period before Stamford Bridge could welcome Peter Kenyon himself, a figure of such importance in managing the strategies – especially financial – that have guided the fortunes of Manchester United worldwide in recent years. This was the first real sign that things in the structure of the club were indeed about to change. I had never met either of them, even if Peter Kenyon was familiar to me by way of the remarkable results achieved at Old Trafford, but it was obvious that on the market-ing and corporate image front, Chelsea had scored a big point in the world business arena. Clearly, when a person of this standing arrives it is normal that each one of us will have had a few private thoughts about what kind of relationship we are likely to have with the new man, and what impact he will have on our situation within Chelsea FC, but on a less selfish note, one can hardly fail to note the decisiveness with which Roman Abramovich acts in the interests of expanding the club.

Shortly after the announcement, I heard from Spanish friends that Peter Kenyon had been a target of Real Madrid, if indeed there were any need for an endorsement of the professional status of the man and the esteem he enjoys worldwide in the top echelons of football. Over the coming weeks, as far as Paul Smith was concerned, and the coming months in the case of Mr Kenyon, I would find out what kind of rapport might develop between us, although it was not the kind of thing that ever worried me. As a manager I am not very accomplished – as my daughter Claudia good-naturedly reminds me sometimes – at political or diplomatic relations. I tend to be interested in substance, not very much in form. I am probably a little out of step with the times in this sense, but essentially I like my business to be on the pitch. I concern myself with the good of my team and doing my job well, and beyond that I look after my family and my own interests, without going after or taking particular care over special relationships that might help my career. I let the results speak for themselves. In this instance, given the fact that these are people chosen by Mr Abramovich, with whom I see eye to eye, and that their respective track records are sufficient guarantee in themselves, it is reasonable to suppose, at least as far as I am concerned, that there will be no problems with the relationship.

Wolves v Chelsea, Molineux, 20 September 2003

An easy game on paper, but experience tells me there is no bigger mistake anyone can make, especially here in England, than to take a result for granted. The determination and competitive spirit we see in the Premiership are not only ingredients that guarantee a great spectacle, but just as much a constant reminder to more technical teams like ours that they can never drop their guard. Wolves, for their part, are a team combining the experience of Dennis Irwin and Paul Ince with the dynamism of players like Shaun Newton and Henri Camara who are able to inject a change of pace. Despite a number of injury problems, the Norwegian forward Steffan Iversen is no slouch either, given the goals he has scored for Spurs and for his country. In the event, I decided to face them with a flat midfield, using two genuine wingers out wide – Gronkjaer and Duff – and a forward pairing of Hasselbaink and Gudjohnsen.

In the end, the match turned out to be a comfortable win, and indeed the only real problem we had was before even arriving at the ground. A few miles after leaving the usual hotel on the outskirts of Birmingham where we always stay when playing in the area, we realized we had left Gallas behind. To be honest, it is quite easy to forget Willie; let's just say that when he is on the bus, then you can be pretty sure everyone else will be on it too! At any rate we could not go on without him (not least because he was in my starting eleven), so we turned back. Everything turned out well in the end, as we won 5–0 after a fine team performance. It was a marvellous display of one- and two-touch football with depth, and the boys played as if attached by a fine thread one to another, so perfect was their movement. Towards the end, with the game more or less safe, we saw two goals from Hernan Crespo, his first in the Premiership, which made me especially pleased, both for him and for us. I know how important it is for a forward to find the net, and

69

how even more important that is for a player coming in from a completely different environment. Not that a player like Crespo needs to score a brace against Wolves to prove his worth, but I can assure anyone that he too was extremely happy with his afternoon in the Midlands. This is a predatory striker, ready to exploit any error made by the opposition defence. He is already renowned the world over for this predatory style of his, but it is good that he should open his goal-scoring account in England too.

The only unpleasant aspect of the afternoon occurred in the post-match press conference. The first question directed at me was: 'Mr. Ranieri, how come you didn't use Wayne Bridge, an English player, in this match?'

What? We win 5–0 away from home, even if it is against a team having a bit of a difficult start to life in the Premiership, and the first thing they ask me is why I didn't play Bridge? *Is this a joke?* I hope so, because otherwise I would have to think that someone is so biased as to find something negative to say even when there's absolutely nothing to find. The result and the quality of our play would certainly not have suggested a controversial first question. And to make the observation that I left an Englishman out of the team, when surely my intention to build the Chelsea of the future with an English backbone has been both stated in words and proven by deeds, seems almost spiteful.

Happily there is always a positive side to everything, and I must say that not even that silly question could spoil an afternoon I will remember for a long time. For the win, certainly. And obviously the score. But this time the reader must allow me a little 'moment' of my own. To see the entire lower part of the stand opposite the dugout occupied by Chelsea supporters was wonderful, and a magnificent sight. A truly handsome splash of blue and white. And to hear the fans chant for me during the match was really quite touching. As my English is still improving, the things that supporters sing and shout in the stadium can sometimes be difficult to make out, but even I could not mistake the one declaring that this is Ranieri's team and we don't want Eriksson. I have nothing against Sven or any other fellow manager, and I want to keep my job only as long as I can produce the results that prove I still deserve to hold down the position of coach to a big club like Chelsea. I have never looked for help from the fans, or the players, or the press. Ingratiation is not my style, and I would rather give up coaching than start pandering for support. But to hear those words being chanted spontaneously did touch my feelings in a special way. I swear I did not know how to respond at that particular moment. Give a wave? A gesture of thanks? I hope no-one was offended, but staying concentrated on the game and simply doing nothing was my way of getting over a minute or two of embarrassment, though I was happy to have experienced it. I have continued to hear the chants ever since that afternoon and this has increased my sense of gratitude toward our fans – the ones who clearly appreciate what I am doing, and whom I hope to repay with big results. The results we all want. If I have never said thank you from the touchline, I do so now on these pages, because this is the way I know best.

The main topic of the Media Day held before our next game with Aston Villa concerned the declarations made by UEFA chief executive Gerhard Aigner, carried by a number of newspapers around the world, which were aimed very much at us. Essentially, he was challenging those clubs that were looking to 'buy' success through big transfer spending and destroying the identity of their teams. Well, if this gentleman was referring to Chelsea he must have been a little distracted, as he failed to notice that I as manager, and indeed the whole of Chelsea FC, were trying to build the future of the club on a foundation of English players. Steve Clarke and Mick McGiven were doing a great job with the Academy, bringing on homegrown players who would be the champions of tomorrow, and we were building the fortunes of the first team around John Terry, who had been wearing the blue jersey since he was 14 years old, as well as Bridge, Johnson, Lampard and Joe Cole, all of whom currently wore the three lions of England. So, given that everyone should look to their own business first and foremost, it would have been nice – and for once I am not talking about my own situation – if people had not relied on clichéd arguments, or if there had been fewer preconceptions when talking about our club. As long as I was manager of this team, there would always be a strong English presence because, as I have always said, a team should reflect the character of the home nation.

Chelsea v Aston Villa, Stamford Bridge, 27 September 2003

An ill-tempered fixture, as Villa have always made us suffer and even when we have beaten them in the past, they have made things very difficult for us. And it was no different this time. We won with a goal by Hasselbaink, who slotted in the rebound from a Lampard drive that Thomas Sorensen failed to hold. But what a struggle. They lined up with a very defensive 4–5–1, although to be honest they should have had a draw, especially as we were well and truly let off by Juan-Pablo Angel on at least two occasions. Both were simple chances, one of which came towards the end. Strange too, because normally he does not make mistakes like that. After 90 minutes the result was the only positive thing to take away, but as for our game and the way we moved, I was not pleased at all. Perhaps after an almost perfect performance like the one at Molineux, everyone was looking unconsciously to have another great game, and in the end we forgot to play together.

The next day, Sunday, I flew out to Istanbul to watch a domestic league fixture involving Besiktas, our next European opponents. Normally I send my assistant manager Angelo Antenucci out on his own to uncover the secrets of our opponents, but this time, since the opportunity presented itself, I decided to go along as well. Angelo and I have always worked together, and there is total professional respect and understanding between us. We see things in exactly the same way, and this means I can always send him and him alone to look at teams and players. Let's not forget that it was Angelo who first 'suggested' I should buy William Gallas. Since then, Willie has become the world-class footballer we know today, but it was Angelo who saw the potential first. He has other merits too, but it would be a long job to list them all, from Cagliari to Stamford Bridge. At all events this was a chance to see Besiktas first hand, and because the Turkish club represented no mean opposition, I wanted to go myself.

Istanbul is a city I know fairly well as I went there for the first time on my honeymoon, and football has taken me back there a few times since. It is a hugely fascinating place with a character all its own. To view the seafront and the fish market, if only from the window of a taxi, and sense the oriental flavour created by the outline of the domes and minarets at sunset, there is a certain magic to it all. We were met and taken around by Mehmet, a former Chelsea player who lives there and naturally was invaluable to us. We went from the hotel to the stadium on foot, and a pleasant walk through the city centre was made even more enjoyable by the hospitality of the people who recognized me. They were all very nice to us, backslapping and smiling. I expect there was the odd jibe as well, but in any case nothing I would be able to understand. Seriously though, the atmosphere was genuinely pleasant and relaxing. Visually, the Inonu stadium is one of the most beautiful in Europe. From high up in the main stand there is a view of the Bosphorus, and it can be stunning, I promise. On a more practical and rather less romantic note, we had a Champions League fixture to get through, and that evening Besiktas were looking decidedly solid. As I watched, they put five goals past Trabzonspor and entirely confirmed my convictions as to the quality of their squad and staff.

Having seen this game, the one against Lazio and the other videos available to me, I decided we would play with a back line of three, matching their formation. My idea was that since we had more quality on our side, we could put them under pressure. Playing 4–4–2 with wingers and full-backs out wide, you always end up having one less player in midfield, with two against three. On the eve of a game, we coaches are always convinced we have picked the right plan, or the winning move, but of course it will all be put into context ultimately by what happens on the field.

On the flight back to London I was musing on the way the month had begun and how it was ending. A lot of imponderables, but luckily everything had worked out well. In fact very well, thinking about it, since not only had we won all our games, letting in only two goals and scoring 11, but more important still, we had played good football. In the early months of the season there are certain general pluses like this – or the return of Petit and the first goals scored by Crespo – which can be more important than winning a game. And it was a month made special on a personal level too, by an award. For the first time, I was voted Barclaycard Premiership Manager of the Month. Definitely a huge satisfaction, in a country where you are a visitor and in a championship as prestigious as the Premier League. A minor event and a major event at one and the same, and both connected with your job. Minor, because individual awards are relatively unimportant in a team sport, yet major because it is so extraordinarily satisfying and makes me truly proud. It's a tangible recognition for the job you are doing. I had honestly not expected it, not least because I never think about these things. Probably because I am always concentrating so hard on things that affect the team more directly. For a coach, the most important achievement is that the team should win, as this is the outcome that repays all the sweat and toil. The true realization of an objective. For example, I never thought I might have deserved this award for any other month of a previous season. So there is no grievance attached to the trophy, now displayed proudly on the mantelpiece in the office of my London home, and it will always remain a wonderful memory, but the best acknowledgement on a personal level will always be to have the respect of my players and the esteem of the chairman.

OCTOBER

'This time no Zone dieting. Dessert!
Well earned, I'd say'

Chelsea v Besiktas, Champions League, Group G,
Stamford Bridge, 1 October 2003

Our first defeat of the season. It had to come sooner or later, although I thought it might have happened against different opponents and in some other way. Instead we lost at home, in a Champions League fixture, and it was a game we genuinely ought to have won. But football can be tremendously cruel, especially in European competitions. We can only blame ourselves and our own mistakes, especially when someone with the class and experience of Marcel Desailly, who would never be expected to slip up, effectively gifted them their second goal.

For the first time in the season, we started with three at the back. This was to mirror their line-up and avoid having a man less in midfield. I was banking on our superior quality, but I had not accounted for ill luck.

After twenty minutes we lost Babayaro through injury, then during the course of the second half, after all my substitutions had been used up, Desailly and Gallas picked up hard knocks and were hampered for the remainder of the game. There had been a few mistakes, to be sure, but in all sincerity I had little reason to reproach my players. We created a lot of chances, and had Besiktas pinned in their own half even before they were reduced to ten men through the sending-off of Ilhan Mansiz five minutes into the second period, and yet the ball simply did not want to go in. Anyone who lives and works in the world or football knows that this will happen sometimes. At half-time, two goals down (soft goals as it happened – the first an unlucky deflection off JT's arm and the second coming after Desailly slipped and fell) and with no more reason to play three defenders, I decided to switch tactics and revert to a sort of 4–3–3 formation with Geremi and Duff pushing forward on the flanks and Lampard and Veron supporting Hasselbaink in attack. It was all to no avail; this was not our night.

To have suffered our first loss of the season certainly did not make me happy, but what angered me more were the attacks from the press, which came to my notice even though I do not read the papers much. In Italy and England alike they were starting up again with comments that my position as coach was a temporary one, mentioning the name of Sven-Goran Eriksson again, and even the name of some goalkeeper or other who might do a better job than Cudicini. Carlo was not at his best, true enough, and people had their own ideas. Some hinted that Abramovich's millions might be used to lure Gigi Buffon, and some suggested a spell on the bench, but it was all nonsense. The reality is that after the game with Besiktas, Abramovich came along to my dressing room with a broad grin on his face. And that was the best comment possible. On the other hand I did appreciate the contribution from Desailly who, speaking as the experienced captain he is, pointed out to the press that this was a close-knit squad and everyone had understood and accepted the new policy of rotation I had introduced. I was once a player too, and I know it is something of a bitter pill to take when you are not selected. That is how it should be. But this made me still more appreciative of Marcel's public statement in wanting to protect the dressing room and the players. A world champion of his standing could not allow a solitary defeat to undermine our prospects for such an important season.

Okay, so we had lost on Wednesday for the first time, but this did not have to be a totally negative event, even if it had put us in a difficult position in terms of qualifying from our European group. The important thing is the team, the squad. I am sure of it and have always said so. One of my worries during the summer was not so much how to assemble so many world-class players, as how to forge them into a productive unit. How to bind together so many prominent individual talents in serving a common cause. Our cause. The Chelsea cause. A team has to know itself well. It's like a family. And everyday life is made up of highs and lows. Or in our case, above all, wins and losses. Getting on with one another and playing well when results go your way can be a bit too easy. It was important for me to see how they would react to their first setback. I would find out at Middlesbrough.

Middlesbrough v Chelsea, Riverside Stadium, 5 October 2003

I could hardly have picked a better set of conditions than these. An away game against an aggressive team, played in front of a crowd that makes its presence felt, like at the Riverside. It was also an opportunity for me to catch up with Gaizka Mendieta, who played for me when I was at Valencia. Gaizka is a very special young man and a fine footballer. Frank Lampard reminds me of him. When I came to the Mestalla in Valencia, Mendieta was a marker who would occasionally go forward in attack. I turned him into an irreplaceable attacking midfielder, who contributed as both goal-scorer and provider. Following in the steps of the great keeper Andoni Zubizarreta, Gaizka was made captain of the Valencia team for his competitive qualities. He was probably a bit too quiet to wear the armband, though I understood he was able to communicate in the dressing room; not saying all that much, but leading by example and through his professional honesty. He was a true Basque. I have to admit that during my time at Valencia I must have heard the sound of his voice no more than three times, because mostly he would just nod, but he was always there when it mattered. We began to talk more when he was no longer in my charge. When he joined Lazio, it coincided with a difficult period in his life.

A season at Barcelona had failed to lift his spirits. Now, in this first week of October we were meeting up again as opponents, and I was pleased to say hello once again, to hear that being in England had put a smile back on his face, and he was happy playing for Boro. It meant he had got over his bad patch, not least his personal difficulties, and I could only be happy for him. All the same, I hardly needed him to prove it all to me by having a fantastic game, as he did, and I had a little dig at him in the dressing room afterwards!

I had based my pre-match talk to the team on a fundamentally important point: 'Taking a fall is not a problem, as long as you can get up again. This is what I want from you today: three points – for sure – but above all to show me some character and prove you have put that Champions League defeat behind you.'

The first half was very good, the second half not quite so good, but in the end we deserved to win and I could come back to London with everything I had asked for. A win and a show of character. A success built on another two assists by Duff and, for the first time, a Crespo decider. Damien is genuinely turning out to be a key player in many ways. He gives me the freedom to adopt different strategies even during the course of a single match, thanks to his multi-dimensional talent. He is a quality player, and if there was a reason I played him behind the two strikers in this game, he illustrated it with those two pinpoint passes, one through the middle and the other, for Crespo, from the right. Mendieta was the pick of the Boro players, but they were competitive to a man and we had to fight right until the end, so that when the 90 minutes were finally up, our victory was even sweeter. Five wins in five away games. We were starting to show some form.

Next, a break for international fixtures – yet another – and this time it could probably be seen to be advantageous, since we would be able to rest a few injured players like Gallas, Veron and Desailly. Once again, though, the rhythm was undoubtedly broken. I had my say on this topic earlier, but the problem obviously keeps coming up. This time, in addition to the need for split training, and the risks of injury and fatigue that accompany trips abroad, there was also a strong psychological factor weighing heavily on all the players who would be involved in decisive qualifying games for Euro 2004. On a personal level, the selfish concerns of the manager were in conflict with the pride of seeing my boys playing for their countries. And I was cheering them on as I watched England's controversial and difficult away game in Istanbul on television at home. It was magnificent to see the way John Terry played such a tricky match with such personality, and pleasing that Lampard was involved in the party too, even if he was not in the starting line-up. I am sure that both of them will be pillars of the national side (not forgetting Bridge and Johnson, and Joe Cole, who are also prospects) for years to come, and I like to think I will have played some part in their development.

With this in mind, I especially appreciated Frank's assertion before the match that he owed all his progress to me. A touch over-generous perhaps, since Lampard has become a player of international quality because he possessed the talent and had the humility to work hard and the will to improve. So it was all his own doing. For my part, I told him when we first met that his attacking game was fine, as he had so amply demonstrated at West Ham. The areas where we had to make improvements were in his defensive play. He would follow a natural instinct that prompted him to get involved in attacking moves, and his sense of timing was perfect for it, but he made me cross sometimes because this exposed the midfield, and as I explained to him, if he was forever darting forward, he would never be able to count on the element of surprise, which in his case could be decisive. Last year, when I used him now and again out on the right, he would continue to drift into the middle, upsetting the team's balance. This year though, with a string of phenomenal performances and goals, he forced me, gratifyingly, to play him in central midfield. Now my only problem was a different one: finding a way to rest him. Almost all observers were united in the view that he was the most vital player, not only of our team but indeed of the entire Premiership, in these first few months of the season. I agreed with them, and it was no coincidence that in statistical terms, he totalled more minutes on the pitch than anyone else in the squad for the season. I knew I needed to rest him now and again, but with all the injuries to our midfielders conspiring against me as well, how could I leave him out?

England managed to qualify for Euro 2004, deservedly so, and Jesper too came back content from his trip to

Bosnia, as Denmark would be going to Portugal as well, but now we all had to concentrate on Chelsea. There was an extremely busy period ahead, and for this reason, seeing that the international fixtures had been played on Saturday, I had called a training session for Sunday at Stamford Bridge, at the very unusual time of six in the evening. A warm-down for those returning from international duty, with something more substantial for the rest, but I wanted them all together so that they could focus as a group on the objectives facing us.

Birmingham v Chelsea, St Andrews, 14 October 2003

It would have been better if we had been presented with a home game following the break, but instead we had to pack our bags once more and return to the Midlands to face a team that was turning out to be a revelation in the new season and one of the sides most in form: Birmingham City.

From this match, I had proof that for other teams, even a home draw against Chelsea could be considered a good result. Being unable to use Mika Forssell for contractual reasons, Birmingham lined up unadventurously with five strung across midfield, playing just in front of the defence. In one sense they had decided not to take any risks, whereas on the other hand – even though we won eighteen corners and had them on the ropes for part of the game – they secured a draw that was ultimately deserved. We pushed forward, but failed to create many chances. Jimmy had a couple, we dominated in attack and had good possession, but in all honesty it was nothing special, and so the 0–0 scoreline was acceptable. It was an encounter that proved the importance of having players who can make a difference in one-on-one situations, like Gianfranco Zola used to do for us, up until last season. Duff and Joe Cole have this type of skill, in that they are capable of beating men and opening up defences, but on this occasion at St Andrews it was not their evening. Despite the result, it was an opportunity for me to say thank you to Steve Bruce, my opposite number at Birmingham, who in a spontaneous gesture had sent me two very good bottles of red wine and a nice card to thank me personally for having endorsed the loan of Forssell to his team. I remember Bruce as the leader in defence of Alex Ferguson's first title-winning Manchester United team, and now I can admire his work on the touchline. Today he is one of the up-and-coming managers of the Premier League, though not that I need to say so, as the results speak for themselves.

A curious incident happened at Birmingham. Before the game, Gallas told me he had recovered from the injury picked up in the Besiktas match. 'Are you sure?' I had asked him the evening before, and on the morning of the match. 'Sure, Boss, everything's fine!' But after the warm-up, just five minutes before the start, he came over and said, 'Boss, I can't do it.' Better than finding out a few minutes after kick-off, but a problem all the same. I had to call Robert Huth down hurriedly from the stands. He changed in a flash, jumped up and down on the spot a couple of times and went straight on. Robert is a good young player, only 19 but with one of the hardest shots in the game. In the not too distant future he will become a very important asset to this club. He is plucky and enthusiastic, and has lots of potential. Even coming on cold against Birmingham, he played his part.

The evening before going to Arsenal was an unusual but pleasant one. It was the day appointed for presenting the football awards. Yes, awards with an 's', because I was expecting just the one, and instead we came away with a clutch. To me they gave not one but two, and there was one for Lampard as well, richly deserved. Frank was named Player of the Month for September, and in addition to the award for Manager of the Month, I received another from the League Managers' Association. I did not know about this second one, so it gave me a lot of pleasure purely as a surprise, as well as for the significance it has: an award for the best results during the first quarter of the season, judged across teams from all four divisions.

The sums are a little complicated as I understand it, but like any award it means a great deal. And among other things I was proud to receive it from the hands of Lawrie McMenemy, who I remember, following the English championship years ago from Italy, as the successful manager of Southampton. I was even prouder still to have received the Manager of the Month award, especially after finding out a few days earlier that it was no less than twelve years since a Chelsea manager had won the award. It is a trophy no-one would ever have dreamt of giving me, had my team not achieved such positive results. So obviously there is great credit to them in this regard. But there are other trophies we dream of lifting. And Arsenal, who we would be visiting the next day, were the team that could stand between us and any trophy we might hope to get our hands on. Preparing for a match against the Gunners is both easy and difficult. Easy, because Arsene Wenger never changes much, and against him there is none of the routine we coaches have to go through before match days, wondering who our opponent is going to select and what kind of formation he will put out. Difficult, because Arsenal are one of the strongest club sides in the world. They have a huge advantage over us. Their squad has been together for many years. Like them, we have plenty of championship-winning players and a similarly long history and tradition, but our situation is different just now because we are still in the throes of building a team. They can go through a season changing no more than one or two players. We have changed ten at a stroke, and it is a process that takes time. That said, one can only pay tribute to Arsenal for all that they have won over the years, and the way they have done it, playing great football. But I wanted to beat the Gunners, not least to avoid the danger of them becoming a sort of bogey team for us. It would have been nice for me this time to have been able to field a full-strength side, but instead I found myself in the hotel the night before the game, looking at who I had available and what kind of defence I could conjure up.

Arsenal v Chelsea, Highbury, 18 October 2003

In the end there was little conjuring to be done. The selections were more or less preordained and I had to adopt a totally new pairing in central defence, using Mario Melchiot and Robert Huth. I felt sure they would be able to do well, even without the intuitive understanding that develops between defenders over time. They did not disappoint me at all, and in fact I congratulated them afterwards, although despite their spirited performance we came away from Highbury empty-handed yet again. Not even a fantastic equalizer by Crespo was enough. I started with a diamond midfield and Mutu and Crespo up front, looking for quick penetration and at the same time providing a defensive pivot with Geremi and Lampard ready to double up on the flanks, where Arsenal are always dangerous. Duff, our trusty provider, played behind the strikers. Then halfway through the second period, when I realized we were not playing well and had lost our compactness, I brought on Gronkjaer for Mutu, who was also tiring a bit, and changed everything around. No more diamond, but four in a line and Duff behind Crespo. In practice, it was a 4–4–1–1. By introducing Jesper I was able to spread the field a little, and above all make certain Johnson had help when covering on the side where Ashley Cole and Robert Pires were at work. A quarter of an hour to go, and the issue was decided by a goal from Thierry Henry. Of course, I accept it was a Cudicini blunder. All too evident, and all too abundantly paraded in the papers and on TV

Don't tell me I look a lot younger in this picture taken during my time at Valencia. It's obviously an illusion!

As a coach, it's always easier to talk to wide players, as they can hear what you're saying. Amedeo Carboni and I were usually on the same wavelength in my pre-Chelsea days.

Don't let this picture deceive you.
Gianfranco Zola and I got on
very well together.

Who's afraid of an English press
conference? When you don't
know a language that well, a
smile will go a long way.

First day at school with the new arrivals. Summer 2003 was a busy time at
Stamford Bridge.

believe Mr and Mrs Abramovich did manage to enjoy themselves on occasion...

We couldn't have had a better start with Mr Abramovich in charge. The Malaysia Cup in July 2003: more silverware for Chelsea's trophy room.

Chelsea v Liverpool, Stamford Bridge, 11 May 2003, and one of the most important goals in the club's history. Gronkjaer's scream says it all – we're in the
Champions League.

Stop looking at me,
Jimmy, and go
that way!

A glorious night in Rome, my hometown, in November 2003. Duff dances over the ball...

...and Gudjohnsen seals our 4–0 win in the Champions League tie. Even Roma fans will be grateful to me for this.

Frank – as Rocky! He deserves the belt for all that he gave me during my time with the club.

Eidur Gudjohnsen was one of the most accomplished technical players I've ever coached.

After that magical night in Rome, not even the UEFA delegate can stop me hugging one of my favourite 'sons'.

So many disappointments against Arsenal. It always seemed to go against us, from Reyes' first goals in England to Carlo's mistake against Henry…

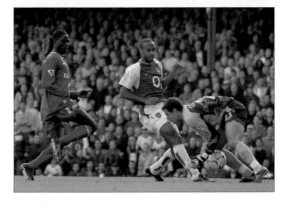

Opposite: No prisoners taken! It's all here in this tackle between Keane and JT: fierce commitment, competitiveness and anger.

Roberto Sassi. Can you tell he's our fitness coach?

I fear many Chelsea fans don't know him well enough, but Mick McGiven's work with the youngsters is vital.

My wife Rosanna and I. It's a telling picture, as I've always lean on her since we've been married

Angelo Antenucci: you can see by his touch that he never played at the highest level!

replays, but I still prefer to call it Henry's goal, in deference to Carlo. How many times has he got us out of trouble? How many miraculous saves has he pulled off in a Chelsea shirt? Enough, I should say, for everyone to realize that this was an accident. It hurts to lose to Arsenal, and especially through a mistake like that, but this cannot allow anyone to forget how much good work Carlo has done. Even in the very same match, just a couple of minutes before the deciding goal was scored. No, this is not meant to seem trivial, but anyone can make a mistake. The problem for a goalkeeper is that when it happens, there is no way back and everyone notices. Cudicini is rightly considered one of the very best, and we must not let his confidence be undermined by what happened in front of the North Bank. I am sure there will be no risk of this, because he has sufficient strength of character, and besides, I saw that everyone had the right attitude in the dressing room after the match, despite the disappointment.

Throwing ourselves back into Europe was the best medicine we could take at that particular moment, and the match against Lazio called for maximum care and attention. Playing against Lazio can never be just an ordinary game for me, as I have already explained, but this time there were many other reasons besides. We had to make amends for our defeat against Besiktas in the previous round, and we could not allow ourselves any more carelessness at home. Also, the test presented by Italian football is always an important one for an English team to take on, and not least significant was the premonition I had confided to Mr Abramovich in our dressing room at the Flaminio stadium after the first friendly played there. Lazio are a fine football team with good players, and are very skilful at closing down space. They are very good tactically, like any Italian side, with an instinctive ability to counter-attack.

Chelsea v Lazio, Champions League, Group G, Stamford Bridge, 22 October 2003

Coming out of the tunnel for the warm-up, my feelings were good. The place was full, needless to say, but I felt a certain buzz in the air. Not that we needed any extra incentive, but one could sense a big-match atmosphere. I stopped to think for a minute. To enjoy the moment. I was the manager of a historic English club competing in the Champions League, challenging an Italian team, Lazio, at home. I had 42,000 fans on my side and a strong team at my disposal. I knew the match would be difficult, but that whole scenario gave me a lift and I sensed we would win. I chose the diamond midfield again, with Duff playing behind strikers Mutu and Gudjohnsen. I had picked these two for their special footballing skills, their ability to perform in tight spaces. They both had important qualities on which I was counting. It also happened that Crespo became unavailable at the last minute due to a groin injury. That was a shame, as it robbed him of the chance to run out against his former club.

In the first half we were a bit cramped, but even

allowing for this, it seemed to me that Lazio's 1–0 advantage was more than they were worth. Simone Inzaghi was the scorer, picking up a sharp chance in the penalty area, but quick as they were in creating and taking it, we had allowed them too much freedom to move the ball from side to side during the build-up. After eight minutes of the second half we had turned it around with two genuine stunners from Lampard and Mutu. After the interval, I saw the character of my team: a phenomenal Lampard (by now the norm) and Veron at his best since donning the blue of Chelsea. It was a deserved and important win. That evening I went out to celebrate with my wife, my brother-in-law and a few friends at a local Italian restaurant, Scalini. As we arrived, Harry Redknapp was leaving. He was very kind. He congratulated me and said he had been so convinced we would win, even when down at half-time, that if a bet had been riding on the outcome he would have doubled his stake. It's always nice when a fellow professional expresses enthusiasm so spontaneously, and even more gratifying when it happens to be someone I admire, as in this case. We had an untroubled evening, good Italian cuisine, a toast with a glass of red wine and – all right let's be honest – this time no Zone dieting. Dessert! Well earned, I'd say.

After a game like this, and above all after a win like this, the important thing is to try and recoup as much energy as possible. And psychological energy is the most difficult to recover. Even with so many objectives in view and all equally important, it is inevitable that a certain element of relaxation can creep in, consciously or unconsciously. So, reassembling at Harlington on Thursday and Friday, our work on the field was dedicated almost exclusively to warming down, although I still tried to keep our concentration sharp. A quip here, a gee-up there, just to keep the squad on their toes, not least in view of the fact that around the corner there were two games in the space of four days, and in my book the League Cup was important too.

Chelsea v Manchester City, Stamford Bridge, 25 October 2003

First up, though, was our Premiership fixture with City at Stamford Bridge. Teams trained by Kevin Keegan are a little unusual and certainly not easy to take on. I do not know him well on a personal level, but as far as I can see, it seems that the former Liverpool legend is particularly keen on attack, and slightly less concerned with containment. This approach tends as a logical consequence to produce highly spectacular, if rather unpredictable games. With a little tactical astuteness on our part, however, City would end up running the greater risks, and this was a point I continued to make during our final training session. Just before taking the field, a few words of warning to Wayne Bridge, who would have to deal with Shaun Wright-Phillips. I like this young man. He has uncommon energy and can be very dangerous when shooting at goal. He covers all the space on the right flank, and gives a good work rate in containment. It is his position that determines how City line up, either a traditional 4–4–2 or 4–5–1. I have seen him play deep in an emergency situation, but my impression is that he gives the best account of himself going forward. He is young, willing and looks to me as though he still has plenty more to offer. His father was a great striker and I am sure that besides being justly proud of Shaun, both he and Keegan – who in the late 1970s deservedly won two European Footballer of the Year awards playing more or less in the same position – will advise him well. Today at any rate, it will be as well for Jesper to keep an eye on him too, when dropping back. And we would have to watch out for their two attackers as well, Fowler and Anelka, even though the former Liverpool star may have had a difficult start to his season. Neither of them are very popular with our fans, given their past histories, though I was hoping that any 'opinions' offered from the stands would not serve simply to inspire them. Fowler had been involved here at the Bridge in a celebrated spat with Graeme Le Saux, whilst Anelka had previously worn the colours of Arsenal . . . enough said. It seems also that in spite of the goals he had been scoring, the Frenchman was not entirely settled at City; indeed word of his future availability even reached us down here. They were a well-matched pair in any event, and we would do well not to allow them any space, as they could be deadly at pace.

We won by a narrow margin thanks to another goal by Hasselbaink, but Cudicini was one of the best players on the pitch, which in itself indicates that we suffered as well. Immediately after Jimmy's goal, which involved a large slice of good fortune – the rebound from a Seaman save striking his knee – Cudicini did exceptionally well to deflect a header onto the post (from Fowler no less). Then with just five minutes left, he managed to preserve the scoreline by pulling off another nigh-on miraculous save from Trevor Sinclair. Not a scintillating win, but a very, very important one because with United losing to Fulham at Old Trafford, we had moved up to second in the table. Given the proximity of Fulham to Chelsea (my own home is in the borough of Fulham), they tell me that among the fans there is a strong rivalry with the Cottagers, but they had certainly done us a huge favour. Now it would be up to us to try and capitalize on the slip-ups of our direct rivals.

By now I am used to the fact that Chelsea is a team often in media headlines the world over, and this does not bother me, but in all sincerity the news item published on that last Tuesday of October was something I would prefer never to have read. Mark Bosnich had been arrested for allegedly assaulting his ex-girlfriend, so she claimed. Obviously I have no idea what actually happened, but I know Mark a little and I know he is not a bad young man. Far from it. He is going through a difficult time, and as often happens in these cases, the problems pile up. I brought him to Chelsea because I knew he was a good keeper, but he has not been lucky. He took some time to get back to full fitness, as he was out of condition when we signed him, then he picked up a string of injuries and came up against a superb Carlo Cudicini, factors that conspired to rob him of the first-team position he thought could be his. There are aspects of his character one needs to be aware of. He is a bit of a bragger and a touch presumptuous, undoubtedly, but never nasty or vicious. I certainly punished him once or twice for his attitude by sending him to play in the reserves, but no-one could ever question his commitment. Physically he always trained very hard, sometimes too hard. He had already starred in winning performances with Aston Villa and with Manchester United, and this probably made it difficult for him to accept the fact that he could improve technically, although he certainly had a good relationship with Giorgio Pellizzaro, our goalkeeping coach. To be honest I would have liked to seek him out at the crucial moment, when the scandal broke. I felt it would be right to do so. But these are delicate situations and one never knows how even the most sincere of gestures may be interpreted or exploited. Whether because of his position or mine, in the end I made no contact, but I was genuinely upset at the way things turned out, as I knew Mark the man and Mark the professional. He always performed better in matches than in training, and I hope he will play again, perhaps in a different environment that is more congenial and less disruptive for him.

Then the next day, we were in all the papers again for very different reasons. According to the press, we had as good as signed defender Michel Salgado from Real Madrid. Our aim at Chelsea was to build a team that would be among the strongest in the world, and Salgado was certainly one of the great players in his position. He was undecided at the time as to whether he should extend his contract with Real. True, he was a player we could have been interested in, with the right timing and arrangements, not least while we were bringing along a talented youngster like Glen Johnson, but as far as I knew at that particular moment, the only contract Salgado was about to sign was with Real Madrid. We would see in due course if anything of substance might happen. For the time being, it was back to business on the pitch.

Chelsea v Notts County, Carling Cup, Stamford Bridge, 29 October 2003

I have made the point already. Every trophy is important to me. Clearly there are priorities, but I exclude nothing. Whilst the League Cup has had its place in the tradition of English football since the 1960s, many of my fellow managers choose to select lots of young players for these games. Not me. I cannot have the team picking up any wrong messages that this is a competition not worth bothering with. Then again, having so many world-class players, anyone I put on the field will necessarily be part of a great side.

I had been amazed to find out that as early as the previous Sunday, our opponents had already sold the full allocation of 3,000 tickets we had sent. Wonderful, but a warning too, in a certain sense, underlining the fact that this was a special occasion for them and we should not make the mistake of underestimating their commitment. I reminded the boys of this the day before, and more especially in the dressing room before taking the field. Notts County has a special place in the history of English football. It is the oldest club in the world, but they are currently in trouble financially, and I am proud that Chelsea decided to lend a hand economically by making a present of the match shirts so that they could be auctioned off to raise funds. I had no intention of giving any discount on the result, however. So much so that I was beside myself in the dressing room at half-time, even though we were leading 2–1.

'Either you start playing a decent match, or I'll keep you here after the game for another two hours watching the tape so you can see all your mistakes . . .'

I said it, I meant it and I really would have done it. Aside from the result, it was all wrong: the attitude, the approach to the game and the way it was played. I substituted Mario Stanic for Hasselbaink after the interval, though I would have replaced the lot of them if the rules had allowed it. I was really angry. We played better in the second half (it would have been almost impossible to play worse), and ended up winning 4–2, which was the best part.

Half an hour or so after the game, as ever, Mr Abramovich came along to my dressing room and together we watched the draw being made for the next round. There we both were with pen and paper, making notes of the ties like real fans. I greatly admire his enthusiasm, which is so obvious even in simple things like these. There was a little longer to wait than usual, because the tie between Blackburn and Liverpool being screened live on TV had run late. We smiled as the balls were picked out. We were drawn with Reading. An away game, though we both knew it was undoubtedly a match we could win. I was not the only one with an eye on the Carling Cup.

A nice way to finish the month, with three wins out of three, after the first four games of the month had resulted in two defeats and a draw. We were not used to results like these, but we bounced back well and for me this was important.

NOVEMBER

'Spitting is a vile gesture, better left to llamas'

November turned out to be a triumphant month, though on paper it was full of uncertainties. Up to that moment we were well placed in all competitions, but with no guarantee of success in any of them, and so we would have to get our heads down, work hard and go into every game hungry for the win.

These were the thoughts and reflections running through my mind as we flew up to Liverpool for the second time in the season. We were going to knock on the door of David Moyes, the determined Scot who has done a fine job at Goodison Park, pulling the Toffees from the mire of recent years and lifting them to a higher level. He had the good fortune to find a pure young talent like Wayne Rooney on his hands, certainly, but in reality it could be said that his handling of the Rooney situation has been the hardest task, and the most skilfully negotiated. In the face of pressure to satisfy popular demand (the fans, the player, the press, sponsors, and the directors and the national team too, I suspect) to yield and make him an automatic selection would have been just too easy, as well as risky for the player's future.

Working with young players is exciting, and it is a delicate business too. The coach has to find a balance between how he wants to use them, and how much he thinks he can expect of them. It is essential for youngsters to gain experience, at a high level were possible, and to take on responsibility. But it must all be done gradually. I have never been afraid to take a gamble on young players in the course of my career, but clearly one has to take account of the situation. A club like Chelsea has to invest in youth with an eye to the future, but equally, and especially at a time like this, it is duty bound to go for players who will enable the team to challenge for top honours straight away. Glen Johnson and Joe Cole, for example, are big investments for the future, and yet able to deliver significant first-team performances even now. At Valencia, on the other hand, having inherited a team well down the table and with no realistic ambitions in the short term, I had no difficulty at all in deciding to sideline certain players – like Romario and Ariel Ortega, who were on astronomical salaries but probably lacking the right kind of motivation – and concentrate on others like Francisco Farinos and Miguel Angulo (and the not-so-young Miguel Soria) who were more hungry. At Fiorentina, my coaching staff were responsible for launching the careers of Francesco Flachi, Franceso Toldo and Cristiano Zanetti, who all went on to play for Italy, as well as Christian Amoroso and

Giovanni Tedesco, who represented their country at under-21 level.

Everton v Chelsea, Goodison Park, 1 November 2003

Everton are a very physical side, and even before lining up on the pitch I knew that we were in for a battle. It was with this in mind that I selected Geremi to start, because even though he was not absolutely match fit, he could be invaluable in a containing role together with Makelele, and allow Lampard to make his forward runs. The creativity I would expect to come from Joe Cole, and the substance from Mutu and Hasselbaink up front.

In the end we won, but we were fortunate. Right from the start Everton had incredible chances. Had they scored in the first half, we could have had no objections. The second half began with a great save by Carlo, and for a moment I was afraid that after a half-time interval during which I thought I made my feelings pretty clear, not much had changed. Then, practically with the next move of the game, it was Mutu who scored at the other end and from that moment, the fourth minute after the restart, the match turned. We had plenty of opportunities to kill it off, but were guilty of not doing so. This is the best way of asking for trouble, and in fact they almost equalized through Francis Jeffers. It really did seem as if the game would never end. At the end of the 90 minutes, deep into injury-time, there was even a chance for us to go 2–0 up, and then yet another miraculous save by Carlo ensured we took home three points. Besides the win, I went back to London with one important personal satisfaction. Joe Cole, one of my – one of our – biggest bets for the future, had been extraordinary. He had done the right thing at the right time, every time. He had been well pumped up and shown it in the best way possible. I was just hoping he would not be the type to be happy with a good game here and there. He would have to work hard and grow, but he has considerable potential and to waste it would be criminal.

We arrived back in London quite late, and I came home shattered, though not because of the journey. I had expended more vocal and physical energy than ever before at Goodison, and this was the clearest indication that it had been a very hard match.

We had a training session at Harlington next day, then we packed our bags for our Champions League second leg tie in Rome, which in my case meant going home. This made it a complicated trip, for so many reasons: the Italian press obviously would want to talk to me for their presentation of the match; the 'goodwill' telephone calls from friends and relations, Roma and Lazio supporters alike (naturally hoping for opposite outcomes); the fact that in your own back yard there are never enough tickets to go round. And the odd situation of staying in a hotel when you have a home no more than three kilometres away. But the most important thing on my mind was the encounter with Roberto Mancini's Lazio team. A successful first leg against them at Stamford Bridge had put our European campaign back on track and we could even have permitted ourselves the luxury of just controlling the game and maybe settling for a draw, but these ideas are not for me. Besiktas had already shown us that in this kind of competition the unexpected is always lurking around the corner, and I only know one way to prepare my team for matches – to win. And we would try and win this time as well.

In the meantime, I had read about growing speculation in the press that we might be buying Roberto Ayala from Valencia. It was not true that he had signed a contract with Chelsea, but it *was* true that we were interested in the Argentinian. He has the qualities that would enable him to adapt to the English game, and is experienced enough to fit in quickly with a top team. Excellent in the air and physically strong, he has played in Italy, though without much success it must be said, held down a regular first-team place in Spain at Valencia, winning La Liga and reaching successive European Cup finals with them, and has been a permanent fixture in his national side for some time. True, he may not be in the first flush of youth, but he is a leader and could be an important addition to our squad. His inclusion would create competition for positions in central defence and above all ensure that in emergencies, we would not need to rely on makeshift solutions. It would take several weeks more to see where the talks might lead, but if the prospect of bringing him to Stamford Bridge was one I certainly liked. It was not destined to happen, though, and indeed by the end of the season Ayala would have aother league title and a UEFA Cup winners medal to his name.

CLAUDIO RANIERI

Lazio v Chelsea, Champions League, Group G, Stadio Olimpico,
4 November 2003

I have a confession to make. Even if my mind was a hun-
dred percent on our game at the Stadio Olimpico, a part
of me was in France with Manu Petit, who was due to go
under the surgeon's knife again just a few hours before
our game would be starting. With his knee continuing
to bother him, he had decided to have the operation. He
was determined to do everything in his power to beat
the problem and get back on the field. He wanted to end
his career in a way befitting the great player that he is,
and as far as we were concerned, quite apart from the
obvious human solidarity, the club had plenty to gain
from his recovery. As I have said many times already, his
recovery remains vital to our cause. Chelsea need him
for all the things he can give to the team physically, in
terms of character, and as a footballer. When we bought
him from Barcelona, I went over there personally to persuade him to sign, and I have never regretted it. I am only
sorry he has had these injury problems, and sorry he has
been prevented from enjoying the continuity that would
have made him a legend at Stamford Bridge and helped
Chelsea to win one or two more trophies. But he had not
given up, and the doctors were confident, so I too could
hardly avoid being optimistic.

Mancini played mind games with his line-up right
until the last minute, then fielded a side different to
the one we played against in London. Neither was it the
starting eleven I expected. He had Luciano Zauri on the

104

right of the back line, probably to keep an eye on Duff, and a midfield with Déjan Stankovic wide on the left and Fabio Liverani in the middle. The Italian newspapers were guessing Mancini would pick a holding midfielder, Giuliano Giannichedda, to close down Lampard, whereas in the event he went for players with greater flair and footballing skills. It was an approach that struck me as being not very 'Italian', but admirable nevertheless.

I decided once again to play a diamond formation in midfield, starting with Veron on the left, Lampard on the right and Duff behind the two strikers. I cautioned Frank in particular not to get too carried away with enthusiasm, not to keep driving forward incessantly, and to cover in defence. In the end I could not have been happier with the result and with the way all the boys acquitted themselves.

It was a great win. And it gave me indescribable satisfaction, for countless reasons. Winning away games in European competitions is always hard, but a team that wins in Italy by a four-goal margin has passed a truly stern test of its credentials. On a personal level, to return home as manager of a foreign club and enjoy a success like this was certainly significant. In my case, going into club management abroad was a choice made freely, not forced by events, and so there is no element of revenge. But there is a lot of pride. Pride in myself and in my players.

As the teams were announced over the public address system, Crespo was greeted by the Lazio fans with whistles. Veron was cheered, and presented with a blue and white scarf after the warm-up. I felt sorry for Hernan, not least because he had done nothing to deserve such a hostile welcome. As far I am aware he left Lazio for Inter – as did Nesta for Milan – because Lazio were forced by economic necessity to sell off their star players, and not because he himself wanted to leave. Sometimes, though, in Italy not wanting or not knowing how to play up to the fans is virtually a crime. I had hoped for our sake, and for his own, that Crespo would be able to get his own back in the one way that forwards know how. And after less than a quarter of an hour, thanks in part to a lucky rebound in front of goal, it was Hernan who gave us the lead. For us, it was a moment that should have sent out every positive signal imaginable. Pity the game was marred by a show of bad temper by Sinisa Mihajlovic, the Serbia and Montenegro veteran. In the end it was to our advantage, as he was sent off at the start of the second half, but it is always disagreeable to see a professional of his experience behave so deplorably. Perhaps London teams are unlucky for him. A few years earlier in fact, following a match against Arsenal, he had been obliged to issue a public apology for racist remarks made to Patrick Vieira. This time he was caught on video spitting at Adrian Mutu and received a lengthy ban from Uefa. Spitting is a vile gesture, better left to llamas. Strangely enough, Lazio had their best passage of play just after being reduced to ten men. Cudicini was magnificent on at least two occasions. On one of them, saving from Simone Inzaghi, I honestly do not know how he did it. Such performances in matches like this confirm my belief that, in him, we have one of the world's best goalkeepers.

In any event, I decided to make changes at that point, introducing Gronkjaer on the right to replace Mutu, who had been a bit upset by the Mihajlovic incident and got himself booked, and switching Duff to the opposite side. Gudjohnsen came on for Crespo, and Cole came on to play behind the Icelander in place of Veron. In practice I had changed the formation to a 4–3–3. Lazio would have to leave a gap sooner or later, and a team like ours could not fail to take advantage. Inside ten minutes we had put another three goals past them, making it a memorable triumph. It was not a faultless performance by any means, but this was an evening when the Chelsea team had shown itself to be an extraordinarily well-balanced outfit in all departments, careful not to leave gaps, ready to break out of defence, but best of all, and most importantly, a team with huge personality.

The one black spot came at the end, when Glen Johnson made me angry, very angry. Glen is young and he lacks experience, we understand. But can anyone be so silly as to get himself sent off in the 90th minute of an away game with his side leading 4–0? I should say not. Suspensions are costly in European competition, and to get one like that makes me livid. And, make no mistake, I let him know pretty quickly.

One of the nicest things about the trip, aside from the result, was the visit of Gianfranco Zola to the Olimpico. And in the dressing room after the match, all the squad made a great fuss of him too. Rightly so, because even though he now wears the jersey of Cagliari, I know there is a big piece of his heart still coloured blue. How I should like to have kept him with us, but at least it was wonderful to be able to share this success with him, important as it was for all of us who love Chelsea Football Club. After the match, some of us accompanied him over to the Distinti Sud sector, which was occupied by our supporters. Some of them had seen him in the VIP stand during the game and naturally chanted his name long and loud. We embraced and exchanged congratulations, which were also in order because thanks to him, Cagliari too had hit very good form and I could see them getting back into Serie A. Maybe this will be his final ambition as a player before going on, I hope, to give the benefit of his experience to future generations who need his professional guidance. It would be marvellous if he could pass on his class too, but that, alas, is an exclusive gift. Before we parted company he also urged me to say hello on his behalf to all the fans back in London, which I did straight away via the programme notes I write with the help of 'Spy', the genial journalist who handles all our editorial projects.

I believe there is no-one, not even his relations, who calls Spy by his real name. Come to think of it, I don't even know his name. He is a good fellow, loves the team, and what I like about him, among other things, is his discretion. Spy obviously has privileged access to the players and coaching staff, at Stamford Bridge and at the training ground alike. But he has never abused his position. There are similar people like this in Italy too. But there are also journalists and supporters who become self-styled champions of the terraces, boasting about their intimacy and familiarity with the players. These are not professionals in any sense. Spy most certainly is a professional. Our fans know him well, as the man with the microphone who officiates as master of ceremonies in the centre-circle at home games, before kick-off and during the interval. During my first few months as manager of Chelsea he was very patient in helping me write the programme notes, something that I will never forget.

Victories can sometimes be as tricky to handle as defeats, and I admit I was wary of the possible backlash from such a remarkable win, which had also been given plenty of coverage in the British press – and rightly so. Precisely because I wanted the test of our success to be more credible, I decided that the team for our next Premiership fixture would be the same as the winning side in Rome, fielded in the same formation.

Chelsea v Newcastle, Stamford Bridge, 9 November 2003

'Chaps,' I began my pre-match talk between warm-up and kick-off, 'today more than ever we've got to play our own game. One touch, two touches, the way we know how. We can be sure they'll come forward in numbers, but they'll also leave space for us to counterattack. So, we can dictate the tempo. But as soon as we see them off balance, we've got to hit them on the break, because that's their Achilles heel.'

There was absolutely no way I wanted us to sit back and wait. I wanted to be sure we were mentally alert and ready to strike with tactical precision at the opposition's weakness. A team forced to do without a player like Alan Shearer is clearly going to be less dangerous, but at Newcastle, as I had warned the team, they cultivate an attacking mentality and I was not surprised when our opponents started off brightly. All the same, I had a clear premonition that when the first chance came to mount an attack we might score, and this practically is what happened. The goal was meaningful too, as it was created and finished by the two wing-backs, who proved to be our extra weapon in their half as well as in our own. A nice move set up by Bridge and completed on the opposite side by Johnson, whose silliness at the Olimpico I had obviously forgiven by now, although for his own good I was not going to say anything just yet.

Up until the clear-cut penalty and sending-off of their centre-half O'Brien three minutes before the end of the first half, the game had been evenly poised and exciting for the crowd, played end to end right the way through. Going in at half-time with a 3–0 scoreline and an extra man, frankly, I could afford to be confident of the outcome. And so it turned out. In fact we went on to make the score 5–0, but as a coach, and as a footballing man generally, I could not help but admire Newcastle's attitude. That old fox Bobby Robson had obviously struck the right note in his half-time talk. Pride. It was clear he had reorganized them in a 4–3–1–1 formation, and they had tried pluckily to catch us on the break. After all, no manager wins cups and league titles around Europe like he has done simply by chance, much less take his country to within a whisker of a World Cup Final. Nonetheless, we had the game in our grasp and we held on tight. If I wanted to be really fussy, I could say we did not move the ball around quickly as we should have done, but if I was looking for confirmation that the Rome game was no flash in the pan, then I had been satisfied with the 5–0 win, the spectacular football and five different goal-scorers. We now had to make room for more international fixtures but at least we could break off very happy with things.

There were the usual difficulties during international week in running different training programmes in tandem, but this time they were mitigated by events in one of the various internationals, and in fact by the England game. Eriksson's side lost against Denmark and I was sorry for that, but from a Chelsea point of view the friendly up at Old Trafford was a notable one. The pride and satisfaction of turning out for your country is important for any player, and in this game there were several of my boys picked to wear the three lions on their chest: Terry, Lampard and Cole as first-choice selections, as well as Bridge and Johnson who came on as substitutes. It was a deserved debut for Glen in the senior England eleven, and I am sure, young though he is, that this will help to develop his career without him losing the right sense of proportion, which is always a risk. And it was nice that Joe Cole managed to score, profiting from his forward position in a totally unfamiliar England line-up, almost a 4–3–3, alongside Heskey and Rooney. Terry and Lampard are permanent fixtures in the

111

England squad now, and in the end 'our' part in the game was even bigger, seeing that it was won 3–2 by a Denmark side including Jesper Gronkjaer. I knew they would all be back at Harlington full of themselves the next day, including Hernan Crespo who had scored for Argentina against Colombia. I could only hope their successful outings would convert into a positive contribution to all the squad as our season continued.

Following the internationals, the player who managed to surprise me in the most charming of ways was John Terry. A few weeks earlier, in the car park at Harlington, I had seen him carefully loading a big package into his car. 'What have you got there John?' I asked jokingly. He showed me the contents: his England shirt from the match against Croatia at Portman Road (he had also finished the game wearing the captain's armband), mounted in a glittering frame with the England emblems at the four corners. 'Well done, JT! Look after it always, it's a lovely souvenir, and framed like that it looks really good.' He looked at me and nodded, then got into his car with a broad smile. What may have been going through his mind at that moment, I honestly could not have imagined.

Now, as we started training again in London, he returned with a gift for me. Mounted in a frame, just like the one I had admired, was his England shirt from the qualifier against Turkey in Istanbul, with a dedication.

To Claudio
I will never forget the man who gave me my first chance.
John Terry

I was about to get emotional, for many reasons. Players at this level are not normally very sensitive, and hardly ever grateful (football is a world where people forget very quickly). His thoughtfulness, spontaneity and enthusiasm touched me. That day in the car park at Harlington, I had made an instinctive and friendly remark on the importance of his personal trophy, with no ulterior motive whatsoever. And he had gone a step further. Professional roles mean nothing here. It is all about human relationships. John got his chance in my team because he earned it, and more importantly he was able to exploit it and hold on to his place. For my part – as any player trained by me at any level can confirm – I have never given an opportunity to anyone other than for professional reasons. What counts for me on the field is professionalism. Nothing else. Many of my fellow coaches like to have players in their squads who they trained at other clubs so they can feel more secure, tactically and personally. I have always tended not to buy players coached under previous contracts at other clubs, precisely in order to avoid personal involvement, whether consciously or unconsciously. Friendships endure and they are essential, but professional liaisons come and go. When I came to Chelsea, my impression of John Terry was that of an English player through and through, with incredible potential for improvement. Now we can say he has an international dimension too, and I am proud for him. I like to compare him to Tony Adams, that monument of English football. Like Adams, John has presence and charisma on the field, and he will be captain and leader of this club for years to come, whoever calls the shots from the bench. He wants to succeed, and has the humility to work at improving his game. On the pitch, he is the one who runs things in our penalty area, but he has also been learning to play the team forward out of defence with the ball at his feet. During the week, before or after training, I would often see him practising 30–40 metre long balls, kicking with both feet, and getting more and more accurate. He has become an automatic selection now for both club and country. I know it is increasingly rare in the modern game to find one-club men, but if John can resist the odd siren-call and stay at Stamford Bridge, he will be the image of Chelsea FC in the new millennium.

That framed jersey now hangs in my private office and is one of the nicest mementos of my time in England. And obviously I hope there will be plenty more trophies for Chelsea to put up there alongside it.

On the eve of the game at St Mary's I became really caught up in the final of the Rugby World Cup. There we all were around the television in the dying minutes, fretting anxiously for the Red Rose, and when Jonny Wilkinson dropped the winning goal the room erupted. And it was good to see, even in a situation like this, that we responded as a group. I hoped we would be able to take that same enthusiasm and cohesiveness onto the pitch. There was something to be learned, too, from the England win we were applauding and celebrating.

Southampton v Chelsea, St Mary's Stadium, 22 November 2003

I am not going to say we stole it, but we were certainly in difficulty for long stretches. More than was reasonable to expect for this away game. Saints are a compact side, with James Beattie always a danger up front, but they tend usually to leave a lot of room at the back and I had felt certain we would be able to take advantage better, and earlier. Instead, the first half was boring to the point that I could almost have dozed off on the bench. Happily, at the start of the second half we found the net, and it was a beautifully worked finish from a give-and-go between Melchiot and Hasselbaink. At this point, having made the breakthrough, it should have been plain sailing, but this is not how it turned out and I have to say that it was my own doing. Yes, I made a couple of changes that turned out to be wide of the mark. These things happen, and my opposite number Gordon Strachan also did well to take advantage and inject some life into the game by making three changes at once, bringing on Delgado, Anders Svensson and Prutton; this changed the look of his team completely, and I had already made my sub-stitutions. So this was another reason we ended up struggling, particularly when Phillips and Fernandes had two golden opportunities to score. They were chances we should not have allowed them, but at least I could be reassured by the fact that we showed character when under pressure. The point is that, after taking the lead, we controlled possession well and there were a couple of occasions when we could even have doubled our advantage, but this we failed to do. We have to learn to kill games off when we get the opportunity. It is certainly nice to learn from your mistakes and still take home the points.

Next up was Sparta Prague, and a tie that could give us the points needed to progress further in the Champions League. A game more tricky than it might seem, since Sparta have several talented players who perform better away than when at home in Prague, as they proved against Lazio. It would be important not to drop our level of intensity, given that after the big win in Rome and the recent string of good results we had enjoyed, this was perhaps the biggest unknown quantity.

Chelsea v Sparta Prague, Champions League, Group G, Stamford Bridge, 26 November 2003

'What I want to see from you,' I told the players just before the referee called us out onto the field, 'is the same spirit we saw from the England rugby team that won the World Cup in Australia the other day. Three points tonight and we can win the group, and we started out this season to win. Qualifying is important, but we can't be content with just getting through.'

The notion of 'never being satisfied' was my mantra to my players. Sparta surprised me a little, since it was clear from the start that they were intent only on drawing, at all costs. They seemed almost not to be interested in winning. They wanted to avoid losing, pocket a respectable result at Stamford Bridge, and then take their chances on the roulette wheel of the final day's results. In the end they would be proved right. The game on the other hand was not a good one, due to their lack of 'cooperation', and there were no goals, although we did produce a few chances. Before the match, I had told both Mutu and Crespo that they must make plenty of movement so as to draw out of position the two Sparta central defenders, who systematically mark man to man. I wanted the team to move the ball around very quickly, as Sparta would always have three, four and even more men behind, and this was the only way to create space. But all to no avail. Partly through a lack of precision, and partly a lack of good fortune, whatever we created we were unable to make count on the scoreboard. No table-topping win on this particular night, but in the end we had what we wanted: qualification for the knockout stage of the Champions League. The first concrete achievement of the season – a small step, yes, but a hugely important one.

It was a confidence boost before one of the biggest and most special games of the season – the home fixture with Manchester United. In a certain sense, for us United are the model, the point of reference, in view of everything they have won, and the spirit they have created. They are difficult to beat, with great strength in depth, but we have almost always done well against them. I respect them for a number of reasons, but especially for their incredible capacity to keep their concentration, game after game, whoever the opposition may be. Last season they had gone undefeated in the league from the turn of the new year. Extraordinary. This is the kind of continuity that every team should achieve. To have any chance of winning this game, we would have to play some great football. There is no other way champions can be beaten.

Chelsea v Manchester United, Stamford Bridge, 30 November 2003

There was a wonderful buzz in the stadium. I know it should probably not affect me by now, but every time there is a big match like this I tend to get caught up in that special atmosphere of Stamford Bridge. This has to be the advantage of playing at home. And this time there was a special moment before the match. Back in London following that famous victory we had applauded so enthusiastically, two die-hard Chelsea fans were here to pay a visit: Clive Woodward, coach of England's World Cup-winning rugby team, and Lawrence Dallaglio, soon to become captain again. They came into our dressing room, met Roman Abramovich, and then walked around the field to a well-deserved ovation from the crowd, with *Swing Low Sweet Chariot*, of course, playing over the public address system. Just writing down the title of the song gives me a shiver. After this, we could hardly lose this match. Not just for reasons of pride, but because we really were in good shape.

Once again I opted for the midfield diamond, with Joe Cole behind the two strikers. The more I see Joe playing

118

in this position I think it could be the best for him. He has more freedom to express himself. He can get forward more easily and play less of a holding role. He is a free spirit, and this is reflected on the field as well. I have to say I admire his willingness to make the effort, and to make sacrifices too, even when I ask him to do something he is not used to, but there can be no argument: when he plays as an attacking midfielder his approach is special.

'OK, chaps! Three important things. All crucial in this match. Be aggressive, stay compact, and keep pressing. We've got to take the direct route as much as we can, because they're always good at getting men back behind the ball.' They were all giving me their complete attention. Primed perfectly for the start.

United decided to play Phil Neville in midfield, but in reality I had expected as much. It is a tactic typically employed by Sir Alex for games like this, and in fact he had already used it against us before. If anything, I was slightly baffled at their decision to play two out-and-out strikers in Forlan and Van Nistelrooy. This season they had often used Giggs or Scholes alongside the Dutchman. I have to say though, that whoever they might have decided to include in their line-up, I felt it was going to be us who would make the running in this game. I'll go further. I sensed we would win. But whatever hunches I might have, that there were still 90 minutes of football to play, against a team full of medal winners.

Against Lazio and Newcastle we had secured important and impressive wins, with surprising scorelines, but I am convinced that our success against United was our best performance to date. We played a really good game, with our forwards pressurizing their defence and our own defence always pushing up. We were fully concentrated, always wide awake tactically, sharp, and reacting well to every threat. And they threatened precious little, to tell the truth, but this was almost exclusively thanks to our endeavour. The game was decided by a single penalty, converted by Frank Lampard. There were doubts from some quarters, but I have to say in all honesty that it looked good, because the contact made by Roy Keane in the area was a foul. These are the matches that can turn a season, on the practical level and the mental level too. Beating the champions is a significant achievement, and to do it by outplaying them while displaying the character of a top-class side is something I hoped my players would be able to reflect on. We would need to take on board this kind of awareness in our efforts to take that definitive step forward.

DECEMBER

'I hope . . . to become the Gordon Ramsay of football!'

This was going to be a month with suitcases constantly at the ready, though not with holidays in mind. A trick played on us by the calendar, and the luck of the draw, meant that all our December cup-ties were away games. Jokingly, I remarked that it would be a good opportunity for our Stamford Bridge pitch to recover its condition. No fault of our groundsman, I know, but in my time with Chelsea to date, the playing surface had rarely been in good shape. This is a disadvantage for us, as we are a team made up of quality players with superior technique, who obviously play to their best when the turf is of good quality.

There has been a lot of development going on at the Bridge in recent years, and I understand – though I am certainly no expert in these matters – that the renovation of the stands and roofing created a few problems with the long-suffering grass. A similar thing happened to the San

Siro pitch in Milan. In my playing days, the San Siro had a perfect surface. But ever since they redesigned the stadium for the Italia 90 World Cup, it has been a disaster. No surprise then, that designers of the new futuristic stadiums in Europe, like the ones built for Vitesse at Arnhem, in Holland, and for Schalke 04 at Gelsenkirchen in Germany, have come up with the idea of a portable playing surface that can be rolled in and out of the stadium for care and maintenance purposes. We were scheduled to play at the new German ground this very month, as it had been designated a neutral venue for our Champions League group match with Besiktas. It would be interesting to see what the Arena AufSchalke is like, and we could even hope that this visit might be a kind of dress rehearsal for something historic . . . but any thoughts like these were not to be spoken out loud for the time being. One cup at a time however, and our first date on the calendar was with the three-handled trophy, the League Cup.

Reading v Chelsea, Carling Cup 4th round, Madejski Stadium, 3 December 2003

This was the match when Neil Sullivan made his official first-team debut for Chelsea, having played a few games for the reserves. When poor Jurgen Macho was injured so badly, we had to find a replacement quickly, and of the goalkeepers then available Neil was certainly the best, and the most reliable and the most experienced internationally. Obviously my first choice would always be Carlo Cudicini, that was unquestionable. But having both Sullivan and Ambrosio on board gave me peace of mind in case of emergencies.

I was really impressed with the stadium at Reading. They had told me that the Madejski was a great place, but I was not expecting a little gem of a ground like this, and considering the club's current First Division status too. They have an excellent manager in Steve Coppell, who I recall as a star player at Manchester United and an England international, as well as some good players who made life difficult for us until Hasselbaink finally put us through to the next round. It was Jimmy who struck the decisive blow, as their American goalkeeper Hahnemann undoubtedly had the game of his life. We did not play well in all honesty, and in the end we were just happy to be in the quarters. Having done the usual post-match interviews, it was time for the draw. We were paired with Aston Villa away, and as ever, some were pleased, some were indifferent, whilst others would have been happier to avoid this particular opposition. I was happy whatever the draw, because any Cup – even this one which some people sniff at, though I fail to see why – is a trophy I want to win like all the rest. So, sooner or later . . .

The fourth round of the League Cup was followed by an away game at Leeds, a fixture I am always wary of because of tricky games there in the past. But first, it's a special PR day. Training in the morning as usual, then in the afternoon, an appointment in Bond Street at the premises of Dunhill, the designers of our clothing as from this season. There was a highly enjoyable early evening cocktail with lots of guests, and apart from myself, we had Adrian Mutu, Joe Cole and William Gallas representing the players. On the way to the presentation I began worrying about Mutu just a little. He is a fashion-conscious dresser, but sometimes inclined to overdo it. I hoped he would understand that this was an official team function and to wear a jacket and tie, but I knew it was unlikely. When I saw him I breathed a sigh of relief. He had put on a smart overcoat with a white shirt, and even though he had no tie, I could see he was also wearing a jacket. When the coat came off, however, I saw he had gone for a pair of very fashionable torn-at-the-knee jeans. I might have known.

Leeds v Chelsea, Elland Road, 6 December 2003

We started the game well, but it was the home team who scored first, and being already very much up for the occasion, this gave them still more confidence. The Elland Road atmosphere is hostile, and a reminder of the battles waged between the two sets of fans, they tell me, during the Seventies and Eighties. On the pitch, games down the years between these two teams have nearly always resulted in at least one sending-off, a fact that obviously does not help to calm tempers. Worse still, this year Leeds were facing a truly difficult situation – courageously so, I must say – and all these things combined to make the circumstances of the match terribly difficult. In the end we came away with a draw, which would have been a win were it not for the splendid Paul

Robinson, rightly named man of the match. Pity about the two points lost, but I was happy enough in the end.

Besiktas v Chelsea, Champions League, Group G, Arena AufSchalke, 9 December 2003

During the run-up to this game, Besiktas were accusing us more or less implicitly of having put pressure on Uefa to order that the last qualifying group match should be played at a neutral venue. In reality the authorities had decided independently, following the two tragic attacks that took the lives of no less than 55 people in Istanbul, that it would be advisable for safety reasons not to play any matches anywhere in the city. The game between Galatasaray and Juventus had also been moved, and I think that in this instance, faced with the image of what we had all witnessed a few days earlier, we were dealing with reasons that go well beyond any considerations of home advantage or the presence of home support. I have already remarked how impressed I had been with their warm hospitality on my trip to watch Mircea Lucescu's team, and I was upset when I saw on television what these people were having to go through yet again – the bombs, the victims, the tears. Sometimes, melodramatically, we describe the outcome of a football match as tragic. But this was a real tragedy. So, I can guarantee that nobody from our club had ever thought of gaining any competitive advantage from those fearsome events. When the draw was made for the first group stages and I saw that the final game was going to be the away fixture in Turkey,

I thought how much better it would be to reach this point of the competition with qualification already in the bag. Now that we had ensured further progress, and with only top spot in our group left to compete for (an important goal nonetheless), playing the game at a neutral venue really did not make much of a difference for us; or even for them, seeing that there were only 335 Chelsea supporters among the 53,000 spectators at the ground. The remainder had come from all over Germany (they tell me that people of Turkish nationality or origin account for 8% of that country's population) and neighbouring Holland, all to cheer on Besiktas.

The Arena AufSchalke in Gelsenkirchen is a fine stadium, and it was selected for this year's Champions League final with good reason, although the turf was rather poor, and too soft. All the same, I was hoping we would be back there towards the end of May. In the end we won 2–0 and it was deserved. I came away very pleased not only with having won the match and finishing top of the group, but also because we had shown we were a team of international standing. We played good football, pressed hard and moved the ball around nicely. I particularly appreciated the effort made by Gronkjaer, who I had lined up more or less as a second striker. He did exactly what I wanted him to do, running into space at every opportunity. I knew that the defender Zago was not quick, but he was still a very good organizer at the back, so I had instructed Jesper to stick close to the Brazilian when Besiktas were in possession, and run at him whenever we had the ball. 'Jesper,' I had told him in the dressing room before kick-off, 'your speed will be fundamental in this match', and so it was in the end. Hasselbaink scored a great goal, and it was good to see and applaud Wayne Bridge's first strike for Chelsea. He had been practising those give-and-go moves in training, often with success, and I had kept telling him he must try to bring them off in match situations too. But I was sure this first goal would not be his last. I stated at the start of the season, well aware of our situation, that I had 21 champion footballers, but still no team. Leaving the Arena AufSchalke, I felt for the first time that we might now have become one. That evening, we did not head straight back to London as we often do after away fixtures in Europe. We had already planned to stay overnight in Gelsenkirchen. It was a splendid occasion for a party to celebrate the victory that took us through to the next stage and confirmed us as group winners. We went to an Italian restaurant, and the quality of the food was truly everything one would expect, given the reputation of our cuisine around the world. There was a wonderful, happy atmosphere, plenty of laughs and lots of bold plans for the future. In reality, many of those grand pronouncements made over an excellent plate of pasta or *aubergines alla parmigiana* were a little over the top, and generated by the euphoria of the moment, but I have to admit that as we raised a glass of *limoncello* in a toast, I was thinking seriously of a return to Gelsenkirchen and to this same restaurant to celebrate something even bigger – though I kept that particular thought to myself.

So it was back to London the following day and preparation for our next Premiership fixture. It often happens at pre-match press conferences that we have a few laughs with the journalists. Maybe they have not been used to my kind of approach in the past, but it does seem to go down well. I even said to them once, 'Come on now, tell the truth: if and when I go, you'll miss me, won't you?' I enjoy a bit of humour with the press. I like surprising them, and I feel we have established a good rapport because of it. This time though, before the game with Bolton, I think I really did take them by surprise. 'I hope,' I said, 'to become the Gordon Ramsay of football!' The comparison may seem paradoxical, but to me it is very significant. When you have money you can buy all the best players you want, but putting them together is another thing entirely. Now I have all the ingredients, but I have to work them up into a super-lative dinner; and like any other chef, I cannot do it all by myself.

But back to the press conference, and continuing with the football-and-food analogy, I gave myself one Michelin star (an informed judgement, as when it comes to choosing restaurants I know what I am doing), but two stars less than I awarded to Sir Alex Ferguson, because his record speaks for itself. And thinking about it, Sir Alex would look really good in a white chef's hat ... Within 24 hours of my little bit of fun, sad to say, Bolton would be ruining our Saturday lunch.

Chelsea v Bolton, Stamford Bridge, 13 December 2003

Our first home defeat of the Premiership season, and even if the team had many valid excuses, we could not allow ourselves the luxury of results like this if we were going to raise our level as intended. I know very well that Bolton have achieved great things in recent years, both in the Premier League and in national cup competitions, and so they are a dangerous side. I watched the game last year when they stunned Man United at Old Trafford with a strike by Kevin Nolan, but even so, losing this game left me a touch disappointed. The opposition fought hard, which is their main strength, but they were also a little fortunate. We tried hard too, but in a disorderly way. The defeat was sealed in the 90th minute with an unlucky deflection off Terry that left Cudicini stranded, although this was not the main blot, as without it the game would still have ended in a draw. The more serious mistake was that we forgot to play as a team. It was a game when we were not physically at our best, and certainly paying the price for our exertions in the Champions League, but we would have to watch out for these slip-ups. At any rate, Ferguson was right to say it would be a three-way race between ourselves, Man U and Arsenal, and from one week to the next there would be a point either way separating us, but for the time being this was all immaterial. It wouldn't be until spring, at the end of March, that every point would become decisive.

14 December 2003

I made a mental note to mention this date, because I enjoyed a splendid evening. Saturday's defeat had left something of a bitter taste, but this honestly was an occasion to savour. I was a guest at the 50th BBC Sports Personality of the Year awards. For me, being invited was in itself a great honour. I had never been to a function like this before and I must say it had quite an effect on me.

I never realized the awards ceremony was so widely followed and so well organized. All the male guests in dark suits with the women in evening gowns, this show of elegance was the best single indicator of the event's importance. There was a welcoming cocktail party, then we were all shown to our tables. I found myself with Boris Becker and Greg Rusedski, and even got to exchange a few words with the legendary Martina Navratilova. But my evening was not all tennis. Seated at the tables near mine were the heroes who brought the Rugby World Cup back to England, and it was a pleasure to be introduced to them by 'our very own' Chelsea fans, Clive Woodward and Lawrence Dallaglio. I also had the chance to practise my beloved Spanish with Seve Ballesteros. I am not a golfer, and not a follower of the game, but I am well aware of his stature and his titles. I was the first one called up onto the stage to be interviewed by Gary Lineker. Frankly, I had expected him, as the programme host and an ex-footballer, to be rather less mischievous on the rumours linking Eriksson with Chelsea and not to take advantage of my none-too-perfect English, but nothing he could say or do was going to spoil my wonderful evening. The next day in the dressing room, people who know Mr Lineker made the comment that he needs watching . . . The only regret I had was that my wife Rosanna could not be with me, as she had a temperature and had to stay home. She is not particularly fond of the limelight, but it is nice to be together on special occasions.

Aston Villa v Chelsea, Carling Cup 5th round, Villa Park, 17 December 2003

An away game at Villa Park is never going to be an easy prospect, but I had some especially positive memories of the ground, and above all the FA Cup semi-final against Fulham in 2002. This is also an area where strange things always seem to happen to us. Things we find amusing when we win, and not so funny if we lose. This year, staying as usual in Bromsgrove just outside Birmingham, there were more surprises. Last time, on the way up to a date with Steve Bruce's Birmingham City, the coach driver was unable to find the road to the hotel. In the end we stopped a taxi and had ourselves escorted there. This time, the hotel receptionist forgot to give the players their afternoon wake-up call, with the result that they drifted down for their 5 o'clock snack in dribs and drabs. And not all of them either, as Babayaro slumbered peacefully on. Not a serious problem certainly, but I kept getting the feeling that because of it, we were missing the right level of tension for an important match. Important for me at

131

any rate. For the boys, I couldn't say. Nobody had done anything wrong, and yet I knew the atmosphere was not as it ought to be. On the way to the stadium, I must say I was gratified to read what David O'Leary had said about me in the local paper.

'It is admirable how Ranieri continues down his own road,' said O'Leary, 'despite all the talk going on, which must be unsettling for him, and he deserves great respect.

'If Chelsea were to win something,' he went on, 'it has to be hoped that they would receive the credit due to them, and that people would not simply say they had done it because of having all that money.'

There is rivalry between football managers as in any other profession, but no-one can understand how a manager feels better than a colleague doing the same job, and this season obviously was an unusual one for me. So they were welcome words from O'Leary, all absolutely spontaneous and sincere. I appreciated the gesture and I thanked him. But there was no gratitude in my mind as we drove into Villa Park. I wanted to get to the semi-final. My plan was to play 3–4–3, giving one half each to Makelele and Lampard in midfield. I always need them, true enough, but I had to avoid overworking them physically. I knew they were tired, and even though they will always want to play, it is my job to give them a bit of a rest. We played badly and Villa deserved to go through. They did nothing special, but they showed they wanted it more than we did. I had told my players to be careful, to keep possession and not give the ball away needlessly, but it all proved to be too much of an inhibition. There were too few long balls, and too many mistakes, especially in defence.

Next day, despite the anger and disappointment at going out of the League Cup, we had our Christmas lunch as planned. Nothing glamorous, in fact we ate in our own canteen at Harlington, but it was no less enjoyable for that. Our chef Nick had prepared everything superbly, with a choice of two main dishes (chicken or lamb), a whole selection of side dishes, and some excellent desserts to end with. All members of staff (except for mine unfortunately, who were either too lazy or too shy) took turns to wait at the table, and the new arrivals who thought they had escaped the initiation ritual of singing a song were now required to do their stuff. At Roccaporena, you may recall, only Glen Johnson had been through the ordeal. Makelele and Mutu now did a turn together. Crespo was a little hesitant, but Desailly helped him overcome his shyness completely, and Joe Cole too. It was something else altogether with Geremi, who put on a real one-man show. He sang, danced and had everyone joining in with rhythmic hand-clapping. It was made even more enjoyable as there were some other young Africans present, taking part in trials for Steve Clarke's Academy, and they got in on the act too. It was a wonderful lunch party. It is also nice that a team – a family, to all intents and purposes – should celebrate such an important holiday. In Italy, and the rest of Europe generally, clubs have an official dinner in evening dress with wives, directors, etc. I prefer it like this: simpler. A few informal laughs, best wishes, and everyone can go home.

Fulham v Chelsea, Loftus Road, 20 December 2003

At this stage of the season, there is no time either to think about Christmas or, mercifully, to dwell on past defeats. Events always take over. Following our first setback of the season in those two back-to-back defeats, we would have our chance to restore some pride in the local derby against Fulham.

In a sense, this was a double-edged sword. As if the injuries to Veron, Petit and Gudjohnsen were not enough, we also had Hasselbaink suspended, and only the day before, Makelele had complained of a high fever that prevented him from training. Still, I had asked for a special effort from him before the match and I knew he would not fail to respond. I also decided to give the captain's armband back to Desailly and to rest Gallas, who I felt was below par at Villa Park. Apart from this it would be 4–4–2 again, with Duff and Gronkjaer out wide and Mutu and Crespo in attack. It was a good game and a good win, not only because we returned level on points with Arsenal, who in the meantime had drawn at Bolton, but more especially because it put us back on track. I know very well that football can throw up bad periods when everything seems to go wrong, and we were going through one of these now, but I also know how competitive my team can be, and I was certain that we had it in us to lift ourselves out of trouble. And we did exactly that in the best possible way at Loftus Road, with a great goal by Crespo and with Desailly's leadership, but in reality it was through a great team performance. Just what we needed. Back in the dressing room at the end of the game I said straight out: 'Well, chaps, I hope you realize that when we play like that – the way we know how – we can win 90% of our games.'

The only negative aspect was yet another injury, this time to Duff, who was stretchered off after just five minutes with a dislocated right shoulder. No foul, he simply fell awkwardly after shooting from the edge of the area. I knew I would lose him for around three weeks at least, and for a player of his importance, it was something we really did not need at this time.

With Duff out for a long period, the thought occurred that we ought to strengthen the squad with some new wingers. We had to establish what was needed both on the right and on the left. Obviously we wanted the best young players from around Europe, because the philosophy was still the same: to improve the potential of the squad with players capable of bringing success to Chelsea for many years to come, as we were building for the future. We sat around a table on the fourth floor of the Chelsea Village offices. There was Abramovich, Paul Smith and myself. It was a decidedly lively meeting, with Abramovich listening intently and when he had no direct knowledge of players, asking me for information about them. Smith took notes, given that Peter Kenyon was still unable to perform any official role in the club's business, whereas my involvement was technical, in other words, to make the choices. For the right flank, the only name I put forward was Sanchez Joaquin of Real Betis Sevilla, whilst for the opposite side I had three: Jérôme Rothen of

Monaco, Arjen Robben of PSV, and Jose Reyes of Seville. Also, given the great rivalry that exists between the two Seville clubs, and to avoid the risk that either one could indulge in 'funny business' were they to get wind of negotiations going on for players in the other camp, I was careful to point out that if we were able to land both, they should be signed on the same day. After our meeting, Paul Smith went to Seville several times, but these are very tricky negotiations and I had no illusions that they could be concluded swiftly, if indeed at all.

True, there is never much time for English clubs to think about Christmas with all the matches we have to play during this period, but when it comes round, it is still the nicest holiday season of the year. Going around the streets of London, it seems almost that they make more of it than we do in Italy. It's a question of atmosphere. You breathe the air of Christmas going out and about. It gets into your spirit. The decorations, the cold, all those lights, and people out shopping, bumping into you with all their parcels. As a believer, Christmas is important to me from the religious point of view, but I still get caught up in the commercial roller-coaster too. The best times are the family get-togethers. In Italy and in Spain, football takes a break, like the schools, but since I took a coaching post in England, obviously our relations have had to come and visit us here. But the atmosphere is still the same. On Christmas Eve we had a big dinner at my home. Apart from my parents, who stayed in Rome this year, we were all there. My daughter Claudia, my mother-in-law, sister-in-law Adriana, lots of friends from Italy, and naturally my close colleagues Roberto Sassi, the fitness coach, Giorgio Pellizzaro the goalkeeping coach, and Angelo Antenucci, my number two, all with their wives and children, who by now are almost part of the family. The real risk at this particular time is that of putting on weight. My wife has many virtues, one of them being her prowess in the kitchen, and on these occasions she has no concept of half-measures. From pasta through to dessert, there was an abundance of delights. And calories . . . At Christmas though, I too get very busy around the home. I decorate the tree myself, and I am always the one who organizes games after dinner to keep everyone entertained until midnight, when the presents are opened. During the rest of the year I have no interest in cards and never play, as I used to in my younger days, but in the festive season I really enjoy it. It is almost a transformation. Normally quiet by nature, I turn into a master of ceremonies on these occasions, holding the bank for our traditional games – *mercante in fiera, tombola, sette e mezzo* – and trying to create the right kind of happy atmosphere so that everyone can join in and have a laugh. This is Christmas after all, having a good time with people you love, while not forgetting the religious significance of it all.

All the same, we have professional commitments, and on the afternoon of Christmas Day we trained at Stamford Bridge before checking into the hotel to prepare ourselves for the Boxing Day fixture with Charlton. Not an easy game, as they had been one of the revelations of the season so far, and because they now had Paolo Di Canio, who can run rings round a defence all on his own. And because it has never been easy for us against them, even if we did win our opening game of the season last year down at the Valley.

Charlton v Chelsea, The Valley, 26 December 2003

A disastrous match, although I sensed even before we arrived at the ground that there was not the right level of tension. As our coach made its way towards the Valley, I turned around at least four times as I heard individuals chattering, joking, chuckling. I knew already that they did not have their minds on the game. At least not as much as they should have. The line between winning and losing at this level is a very fine one, and every aspect of preparation is vital, especially the mental. No team full of medal-winning players, not even ours, can allow its concentration to slip, otherwise it will end up looking foolish, just as we did at Charlton.

I had told them to play the long ball, and to play the kind of game they produced only towards the end. We conceded four goals. A nice Christmas present to wrap up and take home with us. Really, everyone was poor. The defence allowed incredible amounts of space on the flanks. Desailly was outjumped by Matt Holland in the first half, and Bridge gave the opposition the freedom of his penalty area in the second. Errors we would not normally make, but here they cost us goals. We began to pick ourselves up in the final 20 minutes, and after Gudjohnsen's goal the game was almost beginning to turn. Charlton were less daring, having realized there could be danger in the closing stages, and began playing deeper by at least 20 metres, but by then it was too late. At the end I was angry and disappointed, but once again I had been struck by the performance of Scott Parker. I had been watching him closely for more than a year, as he had all the characteristics I like that could turn him into a great player. I knew I would like to have him in my team, and with the transfer window opening again next month, he was going to be at the top of my list.

The team was tired, and the Addicks had reminded us of the fact. Brutally. But frankly there was little I could do with a home game against Portsmouth coming up in less than 48 hours. With all the injuries we had, there was no chance to rest anyone for a game or two. For example, I would have liked to leave out Frank Lampard, who needed a break more than anyone, but with Petit and Veron still unfit . . .

Chelsea v Portsmouth, Stamford Bridge, 28 December 2003

After the defeat at the Valley, the first thing we needed against Portsmouth was a result. The reader will have gathered by now that I always like to get the points by playing attractive football, but there are times that practical considerations must come first, and this was one of them.

We had started off a little narrow, not least because Pompey were giving us problems. They were creating difficulties for us by playing five across midfield, with their three central men putting us under pressure when Geremi and Gronkjaer were out wide. Fortunately they had no real chances to score, just a couple of half-chances involving Yakubu, but we were wobbling rather too much. At the beginning of the second half we began to find the right balance, settled ourselves, and a goal by Wayne Bridge finally made everything right.

It was the first time in the Premiership campaign that I had played Neil Sullivan in goal. The decision was dictated by the injury to Carlo, obviously, but one I was able to take quite happily. Sullivan is an expert and reliable goalkeeper, and following an initial period when he had a little too much weight, he was now back to the levels we all saw him display as first choice for Tottenham and for Scotland. Amongst other things, he made a crucial save in this game when the score was at 0–0, which I became properly aware of only after seeing it on television. Portsmouth had made good ground on the left, and because I was unsighted by a number of players in front of our bench, I thought when the ball rolled clear that it had been diverted by John Terry. No matter. I was happy with his performance, and I had no need to see that particular save from Sullivan to be convinced.

In a team like ours with so many attacking options, Geremi seldom had much opportunity to show off one of his strengths: shooting from long range. He is a tactically important player, above all for the cover he provides in defence, but he also helps build the attack. As proof of his flexibility, when playing in Spain with Real Madrid, he was also used on the right side of the back line. I had played him both in a central role and on the right, but, at least up until this particular moment, probably less than I might have imagined at the outset and no doubt less than he would have hoped. There is no way I could say I had been disappointed with his commitment, because whenever he takes the field he is always disciplined, and he has never spared himself in training. But for a player of his experience and skill, somehow I had been expecting more. Perhaps he had not yet found the conditions that would make him feel totally at ease in his new team, at least on the pitch (in the dressing room, he has bonded with everyone). He has won medals with giants Real Madrid, and in a leading role, so I had to be convinced that it would only be a matter of time before he played a bigger part in our performances too. On this occasion against Pompey, he gave a demonstration of shooting power that was almost surreal. As a spectacle, it was perhaps the best goal of our season up to then. From outside the area, he struck the ball full with the instep, and it was still rising as it went in under the crossbar. A most interesting way to defy the laws of physics. The fans could not believe their eyes, but I was happy for him and indeed for the whole team too, seeing the way they had bounced back from the debacle at the Valley.

Next on the agenda was the FA Cup, another competition I particularly wanted to do well in. On 3 January we had a tie against Watford, away, and I knew it would be difficult, even if they were a First Division side. Considering that the boys were tired and had played two games in three days, I gave them the 29th and 30th off.

In these situations, a little rest and relaxation is at least as beneficial as work done on the training ground.

It was the first time for many years that we were able to spend New Year at home with our families, and it was a wonderful sensation. Coming here to England I quickly understood the importance of traditions, even in football, and have always observed them. In fact they have started to get into my way of thinking about things and organizing my work, and obviously my life as well. I know that many will have missed their New Year's Day match, but I also believe it is better for us that way. Not simply for the sake of being able to break open the champagne in the company of our wives, partners, families and friends, playing cards – or for us Italians, getting our teeth into a slice of *torrone*, or whatever – but because in an overcrowded calendar like the one we have these days, players need to rest for a while, especially at a time when pitches are not ideal due to the cold conditions. On this very subject, at a meeting proposed by Sven-Goran Eriksson at FA headquarters, attended also by Arsène Wenger, Gordon Strachan, Gérard Houllier and myself, we all declared ourselves in favour of a two-week winter break that would allow individuals to recoup their energy and recover from injuries, as well as ensuring that the muscles of players would be spared the lasting impact produced by the winter climate when at its most hostile.

JANUARY

'Where are you going, Sven? . . . That's the way to the players' dressing room. At least wait until summer!'

New Year's Eve spent with our families. Not *too* much merry-making, I hoped, and with the FA Cup just three days away I had to play the part of hard taskmaster and ensure we trained on New Year's Day. I tried to soften the blow by calling the session for 2.30 in the afternoon, but with how much success I am not too sure. We did nothing particularly strenuous, given that the match was just around the corner, and because at this time of year the most important thing is to keep the muscles from stiffening up, as the threat comes not so much from partying and guzzling as from the number of fixtures being played.

On the subject of players and fatigue, I told John Terry the next morning that I was going to rest him the following day and I would not even expect him to turn up. Not only did he understand, but like the great future captain of Chelsea that he surely is, the only thing he asked was that I would let him come along to the match just the same. Group bonding is fundamental if a good team is going to emerge, although the process cannot be taught, much less imposed. John had shown me that if the process was not actually completed in our case, it was at least well advanced.

Watford v Chelsea, FA Cup 3rd round, Vicarage Road, 3 January 2004

The FA Cup has a magic all of its own, which I had heard about and was able to appreciate straight away on coming to this country. However, one of the first things I learned was never to rely on status as a predictor of success – even more so in local derby matches. It was a 12.30 pm kick-off, so we spent the night before the match in a hotel near Watford. In general, I try to minimize nights spent in hotels by the team prior to a match as far as possible. By contrast, in Italy it is customary for teams to spend a couple of nights in a hotel before a game, even for a home fixture. Indeed managers will sometimes order a *ritiro* – 'confining them to barracks', in effect – for no other reason than that he feels things are slipping and he wants to do some extra training and bonding behind closed doors, with his players free from external distractions. I consider it more productive and sensible for me to adapt to the English way of doing things, rather than seeking to impose a different culture on the players.

JT was duly rested, whereas I brought Mutu back

into the attack, as he needed to get a goal or two, and Gudjohnsen, as he had richly deserved to be selected on the strength of recent performances. I knew Mutu had not scored in nearly a dozen games, and it was vital that he should find the back of the net soon, as it would be for any genuine striker. This obviously could have been a big opportunity for him, and in fact the chance presented itself with a penalty, but Eidur pulled rank and it was he who converted. I never interfere in these matters. The important thing with spot-kicks is to establish who is feeling confident and who is not, and no-one can do this better than the players on the pitch. This said, if Hasselbaink is playing, the responsibility for taking penalties will normally be his. The tie ended in a draw, and even when allowing for a number of extenuating circumstances I must say I was not at all happy. True, the pitch at Vicarage Road is virtually unplayable, and on cabbage patches like these, a side like ours is always going to come off worst. True, Helguson's header did not cross the line, but the referee's assistant failed to flag, and we found ourselves chasing the game after only five minutes. All that is undeniable. But I was still not satisfied. A top-three Premiership team should put on a better show and impose its superior strength in games like these. I saw we were suffering and tiring, and now there would have to be a replay. Another ninety minutes which, frankly, we could have done without. Gronkjaer did well to keep our rhythm going, and Johnson too on the same flank, but the rest of the individual perform-ances were a disappointment. For instance we defended

145

poorly, and over the long haul we would have to correct some of these careless habits.

We had not been able to finish off the tie on the day, but we were still in the draw for the next round, and it did not turn out too badly. The winner of our replay would meet the winner from another two sides that had also been unable to produce a result in 90 minutes: Southend, or possibly even part-timers Scarborough. So this was an added incentive for us to take into the replay at Stamford Bridge two weeks later.

I mentioned the transfer market in the previous chapter because decisions on players obviously are not made from one moment to the next, but come January a sort of race against time would get underway. Ever since the English leagues came into line with the rest of Europe on transfer regulations, the mid-season transfer window has been limited to the first month of the year. I had no particular needs and no inclination to disturb the team, not least because I try to be reasonable and consistent in these things. Right from the start of the season, I had continued to make the point that this was a year for laying foundations for the future. But there can be no building if changes are continually being made. Naturally as a football enthusiast, and as a lover of the beautiful game even more than as a coach with the luxury of a generous club chairman to count on, I have to admit to being tempted now and again by the class of such-and-such a player, or the brilliance of another. I was happy with the group I had available and with the job we were doing together, but the manager also has a duty not to miss out on opportunities to improve the team. The margins might be tighter, given the talent we already had, but every available option would need evaluating.

As it happens, we were set to buy the Brazilian striker Adriano from Parma. It was my expectation and everyone else's that he would be a Blue from January onwards, but he was plucked from under our noses. This was a bad blow. It was a setback technically, because he is an extraordinary goal-predator and could have made an immediate difference to our team. And it was a disappointment on a personal level too, with the knowledge that no less a figure than Arrigo Sacchi, whom I have always admired and whose example I used to follow in the dugout (I was known in Italy as a product of the 'Sacchi School'), had been involved. Whether or not his intention had been to act in the interests of Parma, a club financially in ruins by then, I cannot say. In the end, the player was swayed by some skilful sweet-talking on the part of Inter chairman Massimo Moratti, and returned to play in Milan.

But our plans and strategies did not begin and end with Adriano, and I was sure that in the remaining three weeks of the month our efforts would turn up the last piece of the jigsaw that I hoped would make the difference through to the end of the season.

We now had to turn our minds to the upcoming fixture with Liverpool, for which the main worry was the condition of Hernan Crespo. Just as the final training session was underway, he had dropped out, holding one of his calf muscles. It would be disappointing not

147

to have him available for a match perfectly suited to the way he plays. An individual with his international experience is worth something extra against teams that play a continental style of football, like Liverpool and the other sides we come up against in the Champions League. 'We'll see tomorrow boss,' he said after showering, 'but I don't think it's anything serious.'

Chelsea v Liverpool, Stamford Bridge, 7 January 2004

And so the Reds were back at Stamford Bridge, bringing lots of memories with them. Two recent Chelsea victories – one at the end of last season ensuring our Champions League qualification and the other at the start of this campaign with a new Abramovich-financed team – flashed through my mind, both hugely important in the history of our club. Thinking about it, in fact, both were crucial for my own career too, at least in England.

This was a key fixture and it had to be prepared for and experienced as such. I knew perfectly well that they were expert at getting behind our midfield line, and so I feared that if we tried to play four across, we would be in too much difficulty. Unfortunately we were still not very well organized in defence when playing with a flat midfield. This was something we had to work on. I decided to adopt my favoured diamond formation, playing Joe Cole off the strikers, Geremi on the left, Lampard on the right and Makelele in front of the defence. On the morning of the game, Crespo did his warm-up as usual with the rest of the party, the doctors pronounced him fit to play, and so I started him together with Mutu in attack.

Before the game, Eriksson came to see me in my dressing room. He had already been to see Gérard Houllier and he asked what I thought about the prospect of a winter break. I said I was still in favour, as I had stated jointly with him and other managers at a meeting held the previous year after an official Football Association dinner. A smile, a handshake, then he wished me good luck and took his leave. As he walked out of the room, he turned left outside the door. 'Where are you going, Sven?' I called after him. 'That's the way to the players' dressing room. At least wait until summer!' We all burst out laughing, although he did blush a little. But it was a genuinely enjoyable moment, and all completely spontaneous.

I was less inclined to laugh after the game. Crespo felt the problem with his calf flare up after little more than five minutes, and he had to come off. This was regrettable, because it left us all with egg on our faces. Hernan himself, for wanting to play at all costs, the medical staff for giving him the all clear, and me for letting myself be persuaded. For starters, in a game against Liverpool we had wasted a substitution after only a few minutes. But worse still, the risk of being without a striker for a few weeks was a distinct reality. We lost 1–0, but I still went into the dressing room and congratulated the team. We were going through a sticky patch, we were in difficulty with injuries, and the boys had given everything they had. I could not have asked for more.

A coach can get angry following a game and a result like this when he knows his players are in good shape, but not if they are in the state that my team was in that day. Of course I knew perfectly well there was the odd pass that could have been more accurate, or a cross delivered earlier, but when you are struggling, you just pray to God the worst will be over as quickly as possible.

Looking back on December, from the playing point of view the only highlights were the tie at Gelsenkirchen and the away win at Fulham. The rest could be forgotten pretty quickly. These rough periods are also reflected in the way situations just do not go your way. The Watford goal that never was. And in this latest match against Liverpool, the penalty not given for Hyypia's clear foul on Mutu, then Mutu himself hitting the post. I went into the dressing room straight after the game and said to the players, 'You know I'm crazy enough to shout and scream after a 1–0 win if I thought we'd played badly and didn't deserve it. Well, today I'm saying thank you all, and well done.' This was the moment we began to be a unit. We had lost, but I saw them playing like a team. Shortly after leaving their dressing room and returning to my own, Gérard Houllier stopped by and said to me, 'Claudio, that's football. You won at Anfield, and we defended for a win here today.' Perhaps he had forgotten for a moment that we outplayed them at Liverpool, but I embraced him just the same.

Crespo was lost through injury, the game had been lost to Liverpool, and now I was losing Geremi too, as he went off to join the Cameroon squad as vice-captain for the African Cup of Nations. Another lengthy and significant absence, but we will avoid dwelling yet again on the difficulties caused to clubs by international commitments. And neither will we elaborate on the problems I would have to cope with on the tactical front, without Geremi available. Precisely because of the number of names missing from the roster, I was forced to draft in a player from the youth team trained by Mick McGiven. This was Craig Rocastle, and it would give me the opportunity to take a closer look at him. We gave him a shirt with number 41 on the back, and I am sure it will already have become a treasured memento for him. He is a strong boy, and will have every chance of making a name for himself in the English game.

In the meantime, the papers continued to report on our negotiations with Charlton for Scott Parker. I was very interested in the player, certainly, though not to the point of spending silly money as the Addicks might have been thinking or hoping. In addition, I had to come out personally and deny a false rumour that was beginning to gain momentum, regarding a swap for Joe Cole. Never at any time had any such idea been in my mind. If Parker was destined to come to Chelsea, he would have much to offer, but equally, I was not about to forfeit the potential class that Joe could offer once he started finding some consistency in his performances.

Leicester v Chelsea, Walkers Stadium, 11 January 2004

As if there was not already enough pressure on us to get a result after the hiccup against Liverpool, a little extra was added by our very own youth team, coached by Steve Clarke. They had thumped their Leicester counterparts 6–0 the day before! Well . . . if not pressure, certainly some added incentive.

From the way we played, perhaps there was little need for incentives. It was a splendid performance, one of the best away games of the season so far. After such a difficult period as the one we had been going through, a win like this one was really needed. It was a smooth, stylish showing, and with some great goals. Jimmy's quality back-heel put me in mind of Gianfranco Zola. Then, as if the choice of scorers had been left to me, Mutu and Babayaro managed to find the net. When I saw Adrian's shot go in, I breathed a sigh of relief. He had not scored in thirteen games, and it was starting to be a problem for all of us. I have already mentioned how important it is for a striker to keep scoring goals, and I admit I had sent him on in the final fifteen minutes at Leicester to replace Gudjohnsen just so he could get himself on the scoresheet. To be honest, there had also been some games earlier in the campaign when, un-decided whether to pick him or another forward, I had given the start to Mutu so he would have the chance to end his barren spell, for the good of everyone. When a striker is starved of goals he tends to get selfish, some-times forcing unlikely finishes and stifling the flow of play generated by the team, to the point that he becomes a problem for everyone else without realizing it. Babayaro's goal was a beauty too, and it put a nice gloss on our win. He had been having a difficult season in many ways, and this gave a measure of satisfaction.

So, in the end it was all positives, including the confirmation that I had four gilt-edged international strikers available to me, and all four interchangeable, although between Eidur and Jimbo the rapport was instinctive and complete. In a sense, they are the image of what our team could become in time. This kind of understanding cannot be invented in football. It needs time, and plenty of games played together, but when it clicks, it becomes an added value and will never be lost. The Chelsea team of 2003/04 is still a new team, full of players who need to get to know each other, as I keep saying, but once the process has been completed, the quality we possess will allow us to become a phenomenal side. And then obviously there is my role, as the one trying to make the transition as short as possible.

Chelsea v Watford, FA Cup 3rd round replay, Stamford Bridge, 14 January 2004

What a great match. On the field and on the terraces. No getting away from it: the FA Cup has a different atmosphere, as if all the protagonists were inebriated with some special energizer. This time we had home advantage, which is no small matter. Not so much for the surroundings and the fans, as for the quality of the pitch.

I surprise even myself in saying this, as our turf is certainly not the best, although compared to that turnip-field we had to play on at Vicarage Road, it would seem more like a putting green.

I had selected a very 'English' formation, lining up 4–4–2 with a flat four in midfield and Mutu and Hasselbaink up front. Joe Cole was given a start, as at Leicester, because he deserved it, but also because I wanted him to gain confidence and to understand that, even if he had played fewer games than some of the others, he was still an important member of the squad, and not only a prospect for the future.

It was a good win, and our progress to the next round was fully justified. It seemed like a seamless continuation of the performance against Leicester a few days earlier, at the Walkers Stadium: good flowing football, careful defence, and some really wonderful goals. In fact I would give a prize to anyone who can tell me which was the best strike, as a footballing spectacle. Was it Gudjohnsen's, with the outside of his foot? The solo effort by Mutu off Joe Cole's pass to go 3–0 up? Or the vintage strike by Hasselbaink which found the corner of the net? Who can say? The Watford goalkeeper Lenny Pidgeley acquitted himself well enough, as he had two weeks earlier. Ironically, he had played for many years in our youth team before going out on loan – and now he was making his first-team debut for Watford at Stamford Bridge as a Hornet! But as is often the case in English football, the stars on the day were the fans, including the visitors, who even on the wrong end of a four-goal scoreline enjoyed their away-day, continuing to sing and chant with justifiable pride, and plenty of it.

With so many commitments, one coming hard on the heels of another, there was hardly any time to prepare for matches. In the few days between our FA Cup replay and the next Premiership fixture, I had drawn up a carefully targeted programme with the help of my staff, and especially Roberto Sassi, our fitness trainer, designed to ensure that muscles and bodies would take the strain. In particular, I wanted to see how Damien Duff was responding to the spell I had given him against Watford, his first competitive game since the injury sustained in our fixture with Fulham. I cannot say it too often: he is our best link between midfield and attack. Damien had at last recovered from his dislocated shoulder, but I could absolutely not make the mistake of bringing him back before he was ready, because however strong our squad might be, I did not want to be without him during the rest of the season.

We had Birmingham coming up and it would not be easy, remembering the away fixture at St Andrews when not even eighteen corners had been enough for us to break the deadlock. They would be without Forssell, whose progress I was still following with close interest, but City are still a tough nut to crack. I admire Steve Bruce greatly for the way he has managed to organize the team. It is a strange process when successful players like him go into management. Clubs seem quite willing to take them on as coaches, thinking probably in terms of the image-related benefits, but the press and the fans are always sceptical. Apart from Johan Cruyff and to a certain extent Franz Beckenbauer, the transition from star player to star manager has always been difficult to achieve. Statistically, for example, only four individuals – Munoz, Ancelotti, Cruyff and Trapattoni – have ever won European club football's most prestigious trophy as both player and coach. I would never be the fifth (playing for Catanzaro and Catania made sure of that) but I still wanted to bring the trophy to Stamford Bridge.

Chelsea v Birmingham, Stamford Bridge, 18 January 2004

It all went much as I expected. My Chelsea a bit tired with so many games being played, and Steve Bruce's Birmingham still a stumbling block, to the extent that in two Premier League fixtures we had not managed – with all our famous attacking flair – to put even one goal past them. To be honest, we did not play a good first half. We were troubled too much by their hustling tactics, which are particularly effective against us, it would seem. In the end though, I could not be unhappy at the amount of work we got through. We hit the post, there were probably two penalties we were not given, and their goalkeeper Maik Taylor was undoubtedly the best player on the pitch. How he managed to bring off one particular save from a Mutu–Hasselbaink move, I really do not know. So, not too brilliant in the end for us, but we did have them under the cosh. For the second half I replaced Gronkjaer with Duff, still keeping the flat four in midfield, and put Cole out on the right, but it made little impact. Our playing surface as usual did us no favours, although we should really have moved the ball around faster. I had been stressing this point to the players since the beginning of the season, and in fact there have been several occasions when sluggish passing was the main factor in our failure to win certain games. We were obviously going to have to work longer and more carefully on this.

Scarborough v Chelsea, FA Cup 4th round, McCain Stadium, 24 January 2004

Having been told it would be very cold up there on the North Yorkshire coast, especially at this time of year, I had taken some very warm clothes along, whereas in fact it turned out to be almost spring-like. The perfect back-drop for a splendid day. The nicest part was the welcome we received, beginning with the proprietors of our hotel. Nothing like the five-star palaces and luxury suites they spoil you with sometimes. Here we were in a family environment, and they made us feel totally at home. It was almost as if we were in some picturesque spot like Wimbledon Village, but on the seaside. The reception they gave us represented everything that sport should be about. Arriving in the town, going to the stadium the next morning, and then running out onto the pitch for the game, you could sense the joy of everyone there, including the opposition players. Is this the magic of the FA Cup too? Surely it is! But we also had to win the match. We could not make the mistake of losing our concentration or underestimating our opponents, even if they were a non-league side. And history provided the best possible warning in this instance, as they tell me that back in 1989, Chelsea were dumped out of the League Cup by this very same club.

It was a terrible pitch but a fantastic atmosphere. In the end we got through, and that was the important thing, but given the number of clear-cut chances we created, at least five or six, we should have been more efficient. We were fortunate that the referee gave no penalty when Gallas handled the ball in our area, and John Terry too committed a foul that could have seen him red-carded, whereas he escaped with a yellow. In reality we could have gone ahead a couple of times in the opening exchanges, with Lampard hitting the post from 25 yards out in the first minute, and this at least assured me that my players had not let themselves be distracted by the party atmosphere. Then with John Terry's goal, we effectively had our result. I also managed to rest Claude Makelele, as he was very much in need of it, and gave Alexis Nicolas a start on his debut. At half-time I withdrew Gronkjaer and brought on Petit, playing him in the middle and moving Nicolas out onto the left. I was hoping that this would be the last comeback for Manu, in the sense that there would be no further recurrence of his injury and we could count on having a key player fit and available for the remainder of the season. All in all, a great party, a real sporting occasion and worthy opponents who gave 200%.

Training camp at La Manga

I had kept hearing about this place ever since coming to England. I knew that a number of clubs had been there for training, including Manchester United, and I decided to give it a try. We had an extremely tough period coming up, with games arriving thick and fast, and there would be no further opportunity for any kind of organized R&R. So it was right to take a break and recharge the batteries. We might even train harder, but it would be in a situation where the boys could also relax, perhaps play a round or two of golf, and above all it would be in a more agreeable climate.

La Manga turned out to be a very nice resort, and the weather was superb. Whenever we phoned home to friends and relations it seemed as if we were winding them up! Of course we still had to train and exercise, but we were doing our stuff in sunshine and a temperature of 21°C, while on the King's Road it was snowing. I was very happy with the commitment shown by all the team in training, to the point that I decided they should have a day off. What with breaks for internationals, bad weather and a crowded fixture list, it was almost an exceptional occurrence to have a run of three training sessions all together. The facilities at La Manga are excellent: eight football pitches, a golf course, a nice hotel, and the food . . . well, not too bad. The resort is set among lush palm groves and – no great surprise here – many sports personalities have homes there, including David Coulthard, Nigel Mansell, Kenny Dalglish and

159

Lorenzo Sanz. Unfortunately we had a few injury problems. John Terry took a knock to his shin and ankle in a collision with Robert Huth, and if that were not enough, he was involved in a clash of knees with Glen Johnson. We carried JT off on a stretcher and, hard and tough as he is, he was actually in tears. We flew him straight back to London, and back also went Huth, who had a problem with the sole of his foot. Neither was Marcel Desailly able to train properly, due to a troublesome calf.

Equally unfortunate was the news of the draw for the fifth round of the FA Cup, which reached us down at our training camp. It would be Arsenal at Highbury. Not again! It was becoming something of a nightmare, although the thought that it could happen had in fact crossed my mind. I knew I would beat them sooner or later, and I just had to hope it would be this time around.

I had kept in regular contact with the club throughout our stay in La Manga, for news on the transfer front. I mentioned earlier which players were on my wish list, but certainly Scott Parker was number one. Negotiations had not been easy at all, but from what I could gather, we were nearing a conclusion. By now it was only a matter of days, hours even, until the transfer window for this season was due to close, and there were other players still waiting to be placed. A good many teams and a lot of agents had been knocking on our doors – and small wonder, as we can safely say that Chelsea would be the club capable of putting real money on the table, whatever the deal. Big sums certainly, but above all solid cash, and with the problems currently facing football everywhere, Stamford Bridge had become a magnet. This being the situation, I had also been contacted by Oreste Cinquini, who was Director of Football at Fiorentina when I coached there. Cinquini had since gone to Lazio, and he was now enquiring if I might be interested in Dejan Stankovic. I had followed the Yugoslav midfielder's progress from when he first made an impression in the colours of Red Star Belgrade, and never doubted his potential. All the same, I must say I did have one or two doubts about his attitude, as I had picked up the odd backroom comment suggesting he was a player who had settled in the comfort zone after signing a lucrative contract. His price tag for a Lazio administration desperately in need of ready cash would have been even less than the sum being asked for Parker, but regardless of the seed of doubt that had been sown in my mind concerning Stankovic, my first choice was still the Charlton midfielder, albeit at the right price. I have never been involved in the strictly financial side of negotiations, but I still felt duty bound to suggest to Mr Abramovich a ceiling above which he ought not to go, however much I wanted the player. The fact that this was Chelsea, the club owned by a billionaire businessman, should not in my view entitle people to milk the club for whatever it was worth.

A little over twenty-four hours before the transfer window deadline, I handed Scott Parker a Chelsea shirt with the number 19 on the back, and we were all very happy. For the player, it was the chance he was looking for to move onto a higher level, and we had an important piece of our midfield jigsaw. I would now be able to use him perhaps in central midfield, giving Lampard or Makelele a rest, or maybe find room for him on the right. I knew that on the flank he would give me perhaps only 80% of what he could produce in a central position, but it would be my job to decide whether his 80% might not in many cases be worth more than the 100% that some of his new team-mates could deliver. Whatever the case, it was an investment for the future as well, and consistent with my policy of ensuring that the Chelsea playing staff had plenty of quality footballers with British passports. In short, Scottie Parker would add another dimension to the team.

On the same day, I was assured that the deal with Rennes to buy goalkeeper Petr Cech was more or less finalized for next season. There were many people who asked me: 'How come . . . you've got Carlo Cudicini, voted best goalkeeper in all the Premier League last season, and you go and buy another?' True, but only to a certain extent. I had thought long and hard before asking the club to compete with Arsenal and Inter when I found out they were after the young keeper, but even if Carlo is an absolute bulwark in my mind and everybody else's, I came to the conclusion that this was a move we definitely had to make. It was clear to me after going to take a look at him, as it was to Giorgio Pellizzaro our goalkeeping coach, that Cech was the biggest talent among the young stoppers currently playing around Europe, and I believed it was our duty to find out for ourselves if he really would fulfil the promise. Cudicini is a certainty, whereas

Cech is a prospect who could turn out to be better than all the rest. The idea was to have both of them in the Chelsea squad and let them battle it out for top spot in a climate of healthy competition. Knowing that Carlo is a great professional, I could count on him to accept the situation with a level head, not least because – as we have learned at first hand over the last two seasons – a team with our ambitions cannot do with less than two top-flight goalkeepers, given the impact that injuries, outside commitments and suspensions can have on a campaign.

FEBRUARY

'It was just the two of us. What could I expect?
Plans? A kid-gloves dismissal?'

Arsenal. I knew that whatever we might achieve in this month of February, and perhaps during the whole season, we would be judged on the two upcoming matches against the Gunners. They would be important, and probably decisive (the FA Cup tie, certainly), but we had to avoid the mistake of reducing our whole month to this double-header. For better or worse.

The beginning of February also coincided with the first day at the office for Peter Kenyon, the new chief executive recruited by Mr Abramovich. In reality it was a delayed start, as the appointment had been announced some months earlier. I knew nothing of him personally, whether he was fair-haired, tall, bespectacled, bearded . . . I had never laid eyes on him, but his reputation as a successful marketing man preceded him, in the light of his achievements at Manchester United. Mr Kenyon had marketing expertise acquired formerly in the sports clothing sector. And yet, as I understood it, he would have a role to play at Stamford Bridge in decisions regarding the team. I could not make any judgement before meeting him, and in fact I was still waiting to meet him to find out what kind of rapport there might be between us. But there were no preconceptions on my part.

If Mr Kenyon was starting work officially around that time, then we were getting on with our job too, preparing for an away game at Blackburn. They were a team in difficulty, which was odd because I had genuinely thought at the start of the season they might be one of the year's surprises – if not actually an outsider for the title, at least a dangerous side. Yet here they were, scratching around in the drop zone. Graeme Souness seems to me to be a great motivator and he had plenty of excellent players in his team, but with so many injuries, like those to Lorenzo Amoruso, a former charge of mine, and to Barry Ferguson, who might have given them something extra in midfield, whatever plans the manager had must surely have been upset. And when a team put together with a certain kind of expectation in mind suddenly finds itself having to struggle for altogether different reasons, the difficulties are doubled. All that said, we wouldn't be underestimating Blackburn Rovers.

Blackburn v Chelsea, Ewood Park, 1 February 2004

Whenever we go to Ewood Park, in the majority of cases we come away with all three points after a hard-fought encounter with plenty of goals. This was Scott Parker's debut, and so I decided to play with a diamond formation in midfield, putting him on the right with Makelele in front of the defenders, Petit on the left and Lampard supporting the strikers. In reality I had put Manu at the back of the diamond initially, to direct the play from a deep position, but then I saw the team was better balanced with him a little further forward and Makelele in his typical holding role. In the end though, these are matches won normally with heart and stamina more than by tactics, and so it proved on this occasion. It was a real English league game, not least in terms of the weather, with wind and rain to make it all even more difficult, and at the same time spectacular. They played 4–4–2, with 'the usual suspects' (Cole and Yorke) in attack, the speedy Australian Brett Emerton on the flank, and Tugay directing the play. As it happens, in the days when the Turk was at Glasgow Rangers, I had thought about bringing him to England myself. I was attracted by the fluency of his football and his positional sense, but it was an idea I had at a time when we simply did not have any cash to spend at Chelsea. When funds materialized at last, he was already in the Premier League and I had in any case decided on another structure for the team, but having seen his progress in England, especially during his first season at Ewood Park, I must say that I had not been mistaken in what I saw.

In this game, as in others, a decisive contribution was made by Frank Lampard, who was playing behind the strikers for the first time in the season. He scored two and was close to a hat-trick. But the great thing was the way we wanted the win and succeeded. Blackburn had drawn level just four minutes from time, and although I thought we were worth more than one point, they had made it 2–2, they were the home side, and the game was almost over. The momentum should have been with them, but precisely in that instant the team showed me plenty of the character they possessed – and not for the first time I must say. With ten minutes remaining I had replaced Petit with Melchiot, putting the Dutchman in his usual right-back position and bringing Johnson further forward, still out wide on the right, but into the midfield sector. Never for a moment would I have imagined that Glen himself might win the game for us, but his was the goal that made it 3–2. And what a goal! A dink past Flitcroft and a half-volley lashed in from 10 yards. Extraordinary! Once he finds the consistency, Johnson is destined to be a great player for years to come, and at European level too. It will be a headache for opponents, but wonderful for Chelsea.

As for Parker, making his debut for us, I was pleased with him too, though I knew he had a lot more to give. He would have to get used to playing out wide on the right, and to taking on workloads higher than he had been used to previously. He started cramping toward the end, an indication that he was struggling physically, not least because he had not played for more than three weeks. His transfer had been costly all round and in more ways than one.

On the Wednesday before our fixture with Charlton, Peter Kenyon invited me out to dinner. Here at last was an opportunity for us to make one another's acquaintance and talk about the present and perhaps the future. Not that I was desperate to see him, or had any intention of pleading my case for the longer term. It was just the two of us. What could I expect? Plans? A kid-gloves dismissal? Perhaps it was just an act of courtesy? Whichever the case, he had chosen an Italian restaurant to make me feel at home. Naturally I went alone, accompanied only by my less-than-perfect English, but even at the risk of not being able to understand everything, including traps that might be laid for me, it was only right that this should be a private conversation. The finer points would probably elude me, but I would be able to focus on the man. In reality, it turned out to be the most exploratory of dialogues, with one studying the other, almost. This is an appropriate description of the atmosphere, albeit an odd one, as it suggests the attitude of boxers in a ring, sizing each other up during the first round. Is this what we were doing, metaphorically? As always, time would turn out to be the best judge, but I was not there to argue. I had absolutely nothing against him, even though I could be sure that if events should lead to the possibility of my leaving this team at the end of the season, his word would be final. Opponents are enemies, or people with diametrically opposed aims and objectives, whereas we were two employees of Chelsea FC meeting with the good of the team in mind, and we should never forget it.

In preparation for our weekend fixture with the Addicks, I had decided to hold the Friday training session at Stamford Bridge: I like to change the scene for the boys every now and then, just to break up the Harlington routine. That same day, some of the press came out with the news that we had made an official approach to Bayer Leverkusen with a view to buying Lucio, their central defender, for next season. This was not exactly true, although it was certainly the case that we wanted to weigh up all the best available options for next year, with that particular central defence position in mind. The Brazilian was just one such option. He had experience in Europe – fundamentally important for a South American as it eliminated the unknown quantity of acclimatization – and he was a World Cup medal winner. We would be keeping close tabs on him, to make certain our assessments were as accurate as possible with the summer in view.

Chelsea v Charlton, Stamford Bridge, 8 February 2004

Everyone was aware of it, and nobody – press and supporters, partisan or neutral – approved of the decision to withdraw Ken Bates' programme notes. This was the first time in more than twenty years of the club's history that they had not appeared. Now, the match programme embodies a tradition I admire and respect, but it is certainly not an instrument of power. In all honesty, I reckon that if there are editorial decisions to be made, they can wait until the start of the new season. It is a shame anyone had to speak about our team in terms that were not exactly positive, but the only thing concerning me on this match day was that people should talk positively about us in terms of getting a win against Charlton. Even when we had managed to beat the Addicks in previous years, we had never had an easy time of it and never played particularly well. The transfer of Scott Parker a week earlier had of course done little to help relations between the two clubs, especially as the deal had not exactly been a simple one. This time we were able to take huge satisfaction from the outcome, in every sense, with a superb win achieved despite being stretched to the limit. We were missing no less than eleven players, so I had to give our Cypriot Alexis Nicolas his Premier League debut in midfield, and not only was I completely satisfied with the contribution he made, but I also worked him into my pre-match talk to get everyone fired up. He is nicknamed 'Rottweiler' by all the others because of the way he plays in practice games on the training ground, as if he were looking to bite everyone's legs! I told the boys before they ran out onto the field: 'Today I want to see eleven Rottweilers on the pitch, so if they get the idea we're in difficulty, we'll show them we can be as hostile as anyone.' In fact we really were in difficulty, because in addition to the absences through suspension and injury I already knew about, the day before the match I also lost Cudicini with a pulled hamstring muscle and Makelele with a bad back. Neither was I able to play Parker, due to a clause included in the transfer deal. It was more or less the same situation as we had with Birmingham, who were prevented from using Forssell against us, so we could not complain. I say more or less, because in that instance it was a loan arrangement, whereas this was a completed transfer move. For the first time ever, I would think, Glen Johnson started the game as a midfielder, but seeing the way he acquitted himself I am sure it may not be the last. The boys did wonderfully well and secured a fundamentally important result, especially with our title ambitions in view, as both Arsenal and Manchester United had won their games the day before. Mutu was unlucky. In the second half he fashioned a couple of important chances but was unable to convert them. On the first he hit the post, and on the second, Dean Kiely pulled off a quite miraculous save. The win came through a Hasselbaink penalty, but I have to say that they were all magnificent in terms of commitment, energy and common sense. It would be wrong to single out anyone in particular, but Gronkjaer was truly devastating. I kept calling out to him during the game, as he was on the flank near our bench during the first half and able to hear what I was saying. At a certain point he made a gesture as if to say 'leave me in peace', and so in the second half I left him alone. In any case he could no longer hear me on the other side of the pitch. The day afterwards I asked him where he thought he had played best. 'In the first half, boss!' And we had a good laugh over it.

On the subject of laughs, I was amused on that same day to hear about an interview given by Peter Kenyon to Chelsea TV, from which all the newspapers picked up just one thread: it would be 'deemed as failure should Chelsea finish the season without a trophy'. Was this a message for me? Was it an attempt to start dismantling my image in the eyes of the fans? As I told journalists the next day, coaching in Italy hardens you to threats worse than this. What people regard as pressure in England is a mere flea bite by comparison. I was not wounded inside by the statement, and neither did I feel threatened professionally, as I had known since the start of the season what was likely to happen to me. If anything, I was disappointed that the real significance of this season had not been understood in certain quarters, where it mattered. This was a year for laying the foundations on which to build a great team in the near future. Planning is a compulsory process for any team interested not just in transitory successes but in embarking on a cycle of wins. I wanted to win more than anyone, and we would pursue whatever objectives were left open to us as far as we possibly could.

At the end of the Charlton match, the news also came through that Cameroon had unexpectedly lost to Nigeria in the African Cup of Nations, and this meant that Geremi would be back with us shortly. I was sorry for him, but from a selfish point of view, having him available a few days earlier than anticipated could only be good for us.

Portsmouth v Chelsea, Fratton Park, 11 February 2004

As preparation for back-to-back fixtures with Arsenal, another game in midweek, away from home, was not exactly ideal, but this is the reality of the fixture list in England. It was a very cold evening but with clear skies.

173

There were plenty of fans on our side, and an intimate stadium with a splendid atmosphere. In short, a perfect evening of British football. Perfect too because we won, and despite running a few risks, the result was deserved. I started with Lampard a little further forward, Parker and Gronkjaer on the flanks and Makelele, our safety barrier, in front of the defence. Crespo was fit again, but for the moment I kept him on the bench. Without a shadow of a doubt the man of the match for us was John Terry. His defending, together with a couple of fine saves by Sullivan, ensured that we came away not only with the win but also with our 23rd clean sheet of the season. Significantly, the goal that gave us a 1–0 lead was scored by Scott Parker, and I can think of no better way to start off a new adventure than by being on target. It was a goal that summed up everything about Scottie's determination and big-heartedness. And the second was superb. Anyone who knows anything about football will certainly have purred at seeing Frank Lampard's diagonal ball – all of 40 yards – met by Jimmy Floyd Hasselbaink, whose lob struck the bar, leaving Crespo to simply pop the ball into an empty goal. A pity that Jimmy's effort could not have gone in directly, as it would have been his one hundredth goal in the Premier League, and to have bagged it in such great style would have been a reason for added satisfaction. But I knew it would not be long before he made up for it, and with interest.

At the post-match press conference, one of the journalists reminded me of Peter Kenyon's remark about the failure of ending the season trophy-less. 'We won the cup in Malaysia,' I replied. 'Have you forgotten already?' And as they all digested that one with a mixture of enjoyment and evident surprise, I smiled and took my leave.

In the coach, on the way back, I was looking at the league table. With Manchester United losing 2–3 at home to Boro, Charlton going down 2–4 in their derby with Spurs, and a draw between Newcastle and Blackburn, we were just one point off second place and no less than seventeen ahead of the fourth-placed team. Any musings on our position could only be momentary however, as I knew full well that Arsenal were waiting for us around the corner, and they would provide the real measure of our worth. We had to stay very focused; myself first and foremost.

Arsenal v Chelsea, FA Cup 5th round, Highbury, 15 February 2004

Before the first of the two clashes with Arsenal, the papers put out a declaration attributed to Ashley Cole, to the effect that if the Gunners won both matches I would be for the chop straight away. As soon as I saw him in the dressing room I called Ashley across, threatening with a laugh that I was going to work him over. He was extremely embarrassed, and coming up to me straight away, he said in earnest: 'No, Mr Ranieri, I swear I never said anything like that. It made me angry too when I read it.' I was joking with him of course, and it had not upset me in the slightest as I knew perfectly well these were sensational quotes that the press dream up on the eve of important games to add extra spice – even though in this case there was no need whatsoever. I believe he really did think for a moment that I was angry, but then he realized and we had a good chuckle over it. I admire Ashley very much as a player and he is a nice young man. For me, he is one of the most dangerous weapons Arsenal have. I had told my players time and time again 'Remember that they always do the same thing. Eight times out of ten they attack down the left with Henry and Pires, with Cole pushing up from the back. That's where we've got to be careful.' With this in mind I had put together a series of clips to show them, and many of these illustrated precisely the attacking play of Cole. Normally, I show these videos to the players after they have had a bite to eat and before they go and get themselves ready in the dressing room, but in this case, as we had a lunchtime kick-off (Sunday at 12.30 pm) I had decided to show them on the Friday. They last between 7 and 10 minutes, never any longer. In this instance I thought it would be useful for them to digest the information for a couple of days, and there would also be a training session for them to try out what they had seen and what they would have to do in terms of counteracting the threat. As a player, quite honestly, faced with this Arsenal side I would have had no need of any suggestions from the coach. I would simply have made a beeline for Cole and closed him down. Evidently, not even an endless string of reminders from me had been enough for my players.

The day before the FA Cup tie I went about things as calmly as ever, even though I was conscious of the fact that this week we were playing with a big part of our future on the line. And I am not referring to my own job. For me, the team always comes first, and the three games coming up could turn out to be vital for us. If there was any frustration, it was the fact of not having all my top players fully available for selection. But it is results that count, and quite rightly, no-one would be aware ultimately that in the first Premiership fixture with them, I had had to line up Huth and Melchiot as central defenders, and now we were going to Highbury without Duff, Veron and Petit, and with Crespo and Cudicini only half-fit. Our FA Cup record against Arsenal has become a fable, unfortunately. We have not beaten the Gunners in the competition since my arrival at Stamford Bridge in 2000, and never at Highbury, which is obviously our fault, but one also has to pay tribute to a great team. They are very strong, and enjoy the advantage of having been together for many years. The present team is a perfect blend of English and French players. They have world champions like Henry, Vieira and Pires, but as I know for certain, they are a genuine unit. A family. And even when you know beforehand they will always line up 4–4–2, it is to no real advantage, because they are so good at winning every battle on the pitch. You know what you have to do, you practise it in training, you prepare tactically, and they still turn you over. They do exactly what you expect them to do, and they do it so well.

This time I had told the midfielders to move quickly, or not at all. Either push forward straight away, playing the one-two with a striker to set up a through pass, or forget the midfield passes altogether and play the long ball. Arsenal were expert at cutting off passes, or they would play for the foul and then restart quickly, doing you real damage. In the dressing room before we went on, I said to them, 'OK, chaps, remember, watch out even when we get a corner, or a free-kick in their half, because they're deadly on the break.' I put Gronkjaer out on the left because he was reliable there at this stage of the season. He had done really well against Charlton and Portsmouth, perhaps better than anyone, but I had asked him not to stay out so wide in this game, as he would normally do. 'I know I'm always asking for width, but not against Arsenal, otherwise they'll hurt us too much through the middle.' But it would not sink in. I tried switching him with Parker, but Jesper was unable to handle Ashley Cole and so I ended up putting him back where he had started.

We played well in the first half, hustled well and allowed them only one chance: a run by Ashley Cole and a great save by Cudicini. As it happened we were first to score, after splendid work by Mutu. I know many Arsenal fans are not too happy with their goalkeeper Jens Lehmann, but nobody could blame him for this one. It was down to the skill of Adrian, who with his trademark speed of execution, which alas he had shown us only now and then this year, picked up the ball, dribbled around the defender and unleashed an unstoppable drive. Superb! We went in at half-time a goal to the good and this was very important, although it gave us no guarantee of success. 'The pressure's on them now, so we've got to pick up the pace,' I said to them. 'Keep the energy and concentration levels high. Remember. The first 15 minutes will be crucial. This is the moment we need to get a second and kill the game off. So let's have no mistakes.'

For the early stages of the second half I could have no complaints. We started off nicely, but then paid a high price for not closing down Jose Antonio Reyes, who duly equalized. It was a great goal, but we allowed him time to control the ball, advance, get a sight of the target, move forward still further, and by the time the despairing Parker came at him from behind – despairingly, because it was absolutely not his job – he had produced a phenomenal strike. Well done him. But no team can go to sleep like that in defence. From that moment the game changed, and not only in terms of the swing in momentum. I tried to spur them on from the dugout, urging them to persevere. I yelled as much at Gallas, who shouted back, 'Boss, I'm giving it everything I've got!' – and it was true, he was giving his all, in every way possible – but I responded, 'Everyone! Not just you!'

Straight after the equalizer, Cudicini asked to be replaced as he was having trouble with a thigh muscle. We knew he was not at his best and had this niggle, but we had decided to take a calculated risk because in a match of this importance I felt more confident with him between the posts. To avoid too many problems, we had decided that John Terry would take the goal kicks, but at the end of the first half Carlo felt another twinge after making a kick upfield, and when the goal went in he realized he would not be able to carry on. In asking to come off he caught me rather on the hop, as I had already planned to replace the two strikers with Crespo and Gudjohnsen and to bring on Joe Cole too, as extra ammunition. Sullivan had hardly pulled his gloves on before Arsenal scored again, though he was not to blame. This was something that could not be said about Melchiot, who allowed Reyes to ghost into the area behind his back. A player of his experience, with international caps to his name, simply cannot allow things like that to happen. Full marks to Vieira for serving the diagonal pass, and to Reyes for cutting in and beating Sullivan to the ball as he came off his line, but our contribution was unfortunately as decisive as it had been unwitting.

Chelsea had wanted to buy Reyes, and it was against us that he chose to chalk up his first 'English' goals. Needless to say, I am an admirer of his and I know all about him, as I follow the matches of the Spanish La Liga quite closely, but even so, I have to say he surprised me by the way he had managed at such a young age to find his feet so quickly with a big club like Arsenal.

Because of the Cudicini mishap I had had to choose between Gudjohnsen and Crespo as a replacement up front. I had called up the Argentinian at the last minute because I wanted him to deal with his problems a bit better. There can be no place for nancy boys in my group. A player cannot use every slightest setback as an excuse for malingering, even if there is a genuine problem. This time he had cut his foot in an accident at home and imagined he would not be required. But he has a special knack of scoring goals, and we needed it. It was the reason we bought him. I knew it had not been an easy season for him so far, what with a new club, new country, language and team-mates, and a different type of football. And there had been injuries too. Lots of problems no doubt, and all real enough, but since I saw him as a medal-winning player and a man who could help us win games, I wanted to see a little more character.

I sent Gudjohnsen on to replace Mutu, not least because he works better with Hasselbaink, but unlike in the Charlton game, when he had done enough within 16 minutes to be named man of the match and picked up the magnum of champagne that goes to the winner, this time he never got into the game at all.

It was a repeat of what happened in the League fixture at Highbury two years earlier. Ahead initially through Lampard, having suffered Campbell's equalizer we lost our composure and timing, and eventually surrendered the match through a goal by Wiltord. At the post-match press conference, the journalists reminded me kindly that the first in a run of three crucial games had not gone too well. I have baptized them my Sharks, the journalists, but I respect them because I know what their job is all about. I never get angry and never forget to smile. Whether the English press are better or worse than their Italian or Spanish counterparts, I could not say. I have a good rapport with all of them, even knowing that there are one or two who lack respect. My words have been manipulated on occasions, ever since I was a coach in Italy. To my mind, misrepresenting a concept expressed by someone also indicates a lack of respect for the reader.

The journalist knows what you are saying, but sometimes uses your words improperly. This annoys me wherever in the world it is done. Journalists do not live and breathe football 24/7 as a coach does. They do not know all the angles. I can get an assessment wrong or read a game differently, which is all well and good. But distorted quotes I do not accept. Here in England, relationships with the press are completely different. In Italy or in Spain you find football journalists even in the showers. They are at the training ground every day. In Spain, there are even radio programmes – highly successful ones – on the air exclusively at night, from midnight until 2.00 am. One broadcaster has average listener figures of between 1 million and 1.2 million, while another has between 800,000 and 1 million! I made a pact with them. 'If you really must call me, do it early in the programme, because after that I'll be asleep.' To avoid them altogether would be impossible. In England, they come to the match, they are not intrusive and we have a good time at the conferences. Some players have headaches not so much with comments on their football as with the publication of compromising pictures or kiss-and-tell stories, but thankfully this is not my kind of problem . . .

Being knocked out of the FA Cup was a heavy blow. Perhaps I was becoming really 'English', but to me it really is a special competition. I had taken the team to the final in 2002 and I wanted to taste the atmosphere again, this time on the winning side. It was a plan I would have to shelve for a while.

The following Saturday it would be Arsenal again,

and the most important thing at this point was to forget about Sunday's defeat. It was a week when we found the Gunners on the path of our present and our immediate future, but in between the two clashes – FA Cup and Premier League – we had an appointment with the past. A couple of events in honour of Bobby Tambling, who for anyone unfamiliar with the history of Chelsea Football Club is the name of the Blues' greatest-ever goal-scorer. A long weekend in his honour began on the Thursday with a reception at the House of Commons, organized by Labour MP Tony Banks. The next day we invited him along to our training session to meet the players, and the same evening he was guest of honour at a dinner at the Galleria. Much as I love this kind of tradition, I chose not to go to the dinner as we had Arsenal to contend with the next day and I wanted to stay focused. But I was there for the reception, as I really did want to raise a glass of champagne to the health of a player who had contributed so much to the history of our club. And it was wonderful too to be in the company of other Chelsea greats like Roberto Di Matteo and Tommy Langley. It would be nice to have this sense of history and gratitude in Italy too, but there is a question of sensibility involved, something we Italians seem to lack, but which enhances the worth of football in England.

The weekend was in Bobby's honour and we wanted to dedicate the most important of all results to him. A win against Arsenal on Saturday would, at a stroke, both restore our confidence and put us back on track in our race for the Premiership title.

Chelsea v Arsenal, Stamford Bridge, 21 February 2004

This is a wonderful Arsenal side, no question, but I was hoping that their dominance would not start to give us a complex. Today there would be 40,000 cheering for us, and it would be an added incentive to succeed.

I decided to adopt the diamond formation again in midfield, with Makelele in the anchor role and Lampard forward, Parker on the right, Geremi on the left. The game was hardly underway when we were already in the lead. With just twenty-nine seconds gone, Gudjohnsen was wheeling away with arms outstretched. Geremi had been quick to dispossess Vieira and send in an inswinging cross from the left, and Eidur just as quick to profit from a moment of hesitation on the part of young Gael Clichy – his first and last mistake in the match – and slot the ball beyond Lehmann. In Italy, it is one of the many clichés connected with football that scoring too soon can be a problem. I was delighted to have scored so early, especially against Arsenal, and even though the result went against us in the end, I do not see that opening goal as having been the problem. The reality is that we had been performing miracles this season. The way we had managed to put together a group of new and prestigious players so quickly. The way we were playing and the results we were getting. But we also have to hold up our hands and acknowledge that the Gunners have been a better team throughout. They are extraordinary, from another planet. Season 2003/04 has been fantastic for them, and the rest of us can only hope it will be unrepeatable! A season which all too clearly, as Damien Duff remarked during the run-up to our FA Cup tie the week before, was putting our own season into perspective. I would dearly love to beat them, but I have to say I admire them hugely. They have class players, certainly, but first and foremost they are a real team. They are a group that knows how to respond when in serious difficulty, just as they did on this occasion at Stamford Bridge. They had made a slip at the start (probably a lapse in concentration) and it cost them a goal. They were on the back foot against their nearest rivals, away from home, with 42,000 spectators cheering for the opposition. In a derby. And yet, in no time at all they had regrouped and started, even with things going against them, to show which was the stronger side.

Character and personality blended with the class of individual players: the perfect ingredients for a superb unit, and the credit must obviously go to the person who has put it all together: Arsène Wenger. Their prowess is best exemplified by the way they fashioned the equalizer and the player who scored it. Vieira won the ball from Makelele, one of the best holding midfielders in the world, and moments later ran into space and onto Bergkamp's pass to put the ball past Sullivan. It was his first goal of the season, and by no mere accident he had scored it in such an important situation. It was the beginning of the end for us in this match. Vieira, world-class footballer that he is, was not enjoying his best period of form during this part of the season, but with all the attributes that necessarily characterize a player of his

185

stature, he had found a way to take centre stage. After
they had equalized, we made life even more complicated
for ourselves. Their winning goal came as the result of
Sullivan misjudging a corner-kick, then, right at the start
of the second half, Gudjohnsen picked up a second
yellow card and was sent off. Such moments of carelessness are a luxury that no-one can afford against a team
like Arsenal. Edu's goal for 2–1 showed once again
that he was now playing a key part in his team's performances, and not a supporting role as in past seasons. I
like this Brazilian a lot, because he makes himself useful
in different ways. He is an excellent tackler, as often as
not defending harder than any of his team-mates, and
a splendid playmaker. He has genuine Brazilian feet too,
and having found more consistency this year he is
turning out to be an important goalscorer. Edu was the
one who had really turned our FA Cup tie when he came
on in the second half, perhaps more so than Reyes with
his debut brace, and this time it was his turn to put away
the winner. Sullivan had a moment of indecision with the
corner, certainly, but Edu was swift to take advantage.

Sullivan is a good goalkeeper and I am sorry he has
not been able to prove it fully to everyone at Chelsea.
The problem is that he, like most goalkeepers of course,
needs to play regularly in order to give of his best, but
as he well knew when he signed for us, Carlo was our
first-choice stopper, so it has not been easy for him to
take advantage of the chances that have come his way.
Another decisive factor was Gudjohnsen's red card. No
argument about the sending-off: a first yellow for diving,

then a second for a bad foul from behind, right in front of my technical area. Even before the referee put his hand to his pocket I knew what was coming and I knew our fate was sealed. At the time I was really angry with the player. To put the whole team in difficulty like that with a stupid foul – any tackle of that sort in midfield is a stupid foul – and in such an important match, was genuinely hard to accept. Back in the dressing room though, Eidur was distraught and apologized immediately to all his team-mates. I said nothing to him because I knew he had realized his carelessness and accepted all the consequences. And I must say, one of the many things I like about my team and about this group of players is their honesty. Anyone who makes a mistake owns up to it in the dressing room in front of everyone else, and accepts his responsibilities. As this is something I never witnessed before in my time as a coach, I was becoming more and more convinced that we had a very special group of players to build on, and that they would begin to bear fruit next season, with or without me.

In any event, the game was practically over with the sending-off, and even though I tried to change one or two things like swapping over the two wide midfielders (Gronkjaer and Geremi) or sending on Hasselbaink to replace Mutu (a big doubt on the day before the game), it did no good. There were three months to go until the end of the season, true enough, but leaving the stadium after the post-match interviews and conferences, there was a bitter taste in my mouth. The title was perhaps finally beyond us now, and even though this was a season

187

we saw as a stepping stone to future success, I always like to win, so these two defeats to Arsenal were very hard to take.

The wonderful thing about football, and sport in general, is that there is always another day. More so than in everyday life. An objective to achieve. A challenge that can take the mind off previous disappointments. For us, this opportunity for redemption was the Champions League, but Stuttgart would provide particularly tough opposition.

In our training the previous month, we had concentrated particularly on going forward as a way of combating the Gunners, but now we went back to working on possession so we could play at our own kind of rhythm. With this match in view I had split the team into groups – first the wide players (wing-halves and backs), then the central (two defenders, two midfielders and the two strikers) – to work more thoroughly on the tactical side and sharpen everyone's attention. Big matches are won not least by getting the details right, and with this European clash coming up I wanted to be sure my players would miss absolutely nothing, and maintain the right level of concentration.

VfB Stuttgart v Chelsea, Champions League Round of 16, 1st Leg, Gottlieb-Daimler Stadion, 25 February 2004

On the night before the game I went to sleep happy. Having watched the video of the only game Felix Magath's side had lost at home, against Bayer Leverkusen before the Christmas break, I laid back and had a browse through the Uefa *Champions* magazine. There, I read that of the teams qualified for the round of sixteen, Chelsea had recorded the highest level of ball possession overall, at 58%. The numbers were comforting, as they confirmed the value of the work we had been doing and showed we were on the right track. I knew we had to improve many aspects of our game and that there was plenty of work to do, but the team was following my lead, and this was fundamentally important.

Stuttgart are genuinely tough opponents and I really believed that our chances were no better than 50–50. They were not a team full of stars capable of lighting up the imagination of football enthusiasts around the world, but they were compact and solid. From this point of view, they were the best in the Bundesliga in my opinion. They could be dangerous down the left with Lahm and Hleb, but had a style of play similar to what we see in the Premiership, and for us this would be an advantage. But there are no easy games at this level, and we simply had to go out looking for a win. I was not worried that the back-to-back defeats against Arsenal would affect us too much, but we nonetheless had to show character in this regard.

The match was one of our best of the season in terms of concentration and tactical application. At first sight perhaps it might not have looked like a great performance, but after watching it again in the hotel later on I was actually very pleased. Indeed I was full of hope, seeing the way we had kept the right distances between

189

sectors and then, after their own goal, controlled the game and allowed them nothing. True, we might have been a little more attack-minded in our approach, but at this level and at this stage of the tournament, it is sometimes more important to concentrate on being practical. Amongst other things, they were particularly good in the air, and when selecting my strikers for the return leg I would need to think about height, given the physical stature of their central defenders Fernando Meira and Marcelo Bordon. Having Duff back was crucial for us. Not that he did anything special, to be honest, but just the fact of seeing him on the field was so important. We had missed him enormously in previous weeks and I just prayed that nothing else would happen to him for the remainder of the season. More than the Achilles tendon that had kept him out for these last few weeks, it was the dislocation of his shoulder at the end of December that worried me, especially in a contact sport like football. We had even sent him to martial arts classes in the hope that he could learn to protect himself when falling, although it is hard to say whether this will be enough. A bit of luck is needed too. Quite apart from being a player of real pedigree, he is also a splendid young man and deserves all the good fortune that comes his way. And it would mean we could have one of our best weapons available to us, through to the end of the season. These reflections on Damien might appear to conflict with the fact that, around the time of the Stuttgart trip, we were also finalizing a deal for Arjen Robben to come to Stamford Bridge next year. But it is not necessarily a conflict. A team with Chelsea's ambitions must have a big squad made up of top-flight players, even if this creates problems of rotation for the coach. In addition, Robben is one of the biggest young talents currently playing in Europe, and these are our targets in the transfer market. But Damien had nothing to fear. He was one of the most important members of the team, and thanks to his flexibility he could even be used in combination with Robben, playing behind the strikers, or perhaps on the opposite flank, from where he could cut infield and shoot on his left foot.

The Stuttgart game was on Wednesday. We landed in London on the Thursday at lunchtime, went straight to Harlington for a warm-down session, and on the Friday we were at Heathrow again, boarding a flight for Manchester. It was a period when we seemed to be spending more time at airports than on the pitch.

Manchester City v Chelsea, City of Manchester Stadium, 28 February 2004

It was a wintry day for our first visit to City's new stadium. I like the old stadiums where you can breathe the history and tradition of English football, but one can hardly fail to admire new ones like this. It may not have the atmosphere of Maine Road, but the City of Manchester stadium is a splendid facility, and with an enviable playing surface.

We won, though without playing particularly well, it must be said. We did well to carve out a couple of

191

chances and in the end we scored through Gudjohnsen, but we had our let-offs too, especially when Fowler wasted an opportunity similar to the one taken by Reyes to put us out of the FA Cup. Glen Johnson went to sleep a little on this occasion, but fortunately the one-time Liverpool marksman was off-target, as evidently seems to be the rule whenever he finds himself in front of a Chelsea goal.

I had decided to give the boys three days off after this game, so they could relax a little following the pressure, the travelling, the matches and the training sessions of these last few weeks. We would be meeting again on Wednesday, and with this in mind I had planned to try and catch the last flight from London to Rome at 7.40 pm so as to spend an extra evening with my daughter in the capital. The idea was to do the post-match interview more or less immediately after the final whistle and have a cab waiting. Just this once I would be leaving the stadium before the players, and in any case they were each making their own plans as to how they would make the most of the time off. After I had finished with the journalists, I was collecting my trolley from the dressing room when Abramovich came in to see me, as usual. We talked about the game and about the things that were coming up in the immediate future, then jokingly I said: 'Roman, I don't suppose you could give me a lift back to London in your jet?'

'Sorry,' he replied, 'but I'm going to Moscow.' Still with a smile, I asked whether or not the route might take in Rome? Obviously I knew quite well it did not, but we had won our fixture and I wanted to round off the day on a light-hearted note. He looked at me and said, 'Get in the car with me and I'll think about it.' Once in the car he phoned the captain and asked him to enquire about the possibility of flying via Rome. Believe it or not, he took me to Rome. What a man! During the flight we chatted about various things, and naturally about the future. In fact for the first time, we were addressing the inevitable question head on. Just the two of us. Frankly and openly.

'Roman, I don't want to force any decision on your part, but ever since you became owner of Chelsea, as I told you on day one, I'm quite prepared in my mind for the possibility that you may want to make changes. All I'm asking is that you tell me as soon as any decision is made, so I can get myself organized.'

In this job we have to seize the moment, and although I would never leave Chelsea if it was up to me, I have to be prepared for the eventuality and ready to look at other options. I had not said all this in an attempt to make a case or put him on the spot. It was simply a question of a professional relationship that needed to be dealt with . . . professionally.

'Claudio,' he said, 'I assure you no decision has been taken one way or the other, and I have never personally entertained the idea of replacing you, but if anything should happen we'll talk about it straight away.'

In the end I was neither reassured nor alarmed by our conversation: partly because, in reality, he had told me nothing, and partly because I was perhaps not seeking any particular assurances anyway. All I wanted was to do my job diligently and achieve something concrete at the end of it – whether it be a trophy (ideally) or simply a best-ever result for the club. If anything, I had to appreciate yet again that I had a good relationship with Roman Abramovich, whatever the future might bring. He is a pleasant man and an ideal club chairman, not just for the money he invests in the team but above all because he has never – and I repeat, *never* – tried to influence my technical and tactical decisions. What club owner does not impose his preferences or at least make them known, either directly or through the press? Take Lorenzo Sanz, the former President of Real Madrid. Did he or did he not push for the selection of his son in the team, ultimately forcing Fabio Capello to quit? And what about Silvio Berlusconi, who publicly forced Carlo Ancelotti into including two strikers in his AC Milan line-up? Not to mention Massimo Moratti of Inter, who as President was forever openly singing the praises of the Uruguayan Alvaro 'El Chino' Recoba. Well, Mr Abramovich never indulged in any of this kind of thing, and I respected him for that.

MARCH

*'Hernan is cross with me . . . but the reason
I left him on the bench is because you
never give him the ball!'*

We had been knocked out of the FA Cup, but elsewhere
we were still well in the hunt, and the coming weeks
could be decisive with the Champions League in mind,
certainly, but in the Premiership too. It was obvious that
Arsenal had a big advantage over the rest, and it would be
pretty much impossible to overhaul them unless they were
to suffer a dip in form, but as I told the boys, we had to
get ourselves into a position that would ensure we never
had any regrets. We had to be right there, ready to take
advantage of any lapse the Gunners might have. We
needed to put them under pressure, make it clear that
we would keep them in our sights, even if from a distance.
In any event this kind of mentality would help us to grow
as a team, and, if the Premiership title really was going to
end up at Highbury, to finish in second place behind them
would be a minimum objective.

I always want to win and I know better than anyone that the history of football, reflected in the records of clubs and our individual careers, is all about trophies and certainly not placings, but in our case the situation was slightly different. Chelsea are a club that had never reached these heights in recent years, even with great players at Stamford Bridge. We would always come close, but never quite hit the top spot. Now the moment had arrived to end the season on a high not achieved since 1955. Rewriting the history books is always a wonderful thing to do, and if Arsenal were not going to do us any favours (frankly, none were expected), it meant we would have to be content with a tale of deeds rather than of conquests.

In the meantime we were continuing to plan for the future, and on 2 March, after the usual medicals, we announced officially that Arjen Robben had joined the club. I have already mentioned that the deal with PSV had been as good as done a couple of weeks earlier, but this was the important part: signatures on paper. The newspapers were talking about a fee of around £9 million, and a five-year contract. For me as coach the interest was purely technical, and this young Dutchman was one of the players at the top of my wish-list, as I hinted in the previous chapter. He would be coming in after a difficult period in terms of health, we knew. During 2003 he had suffered a scare when doctors diagnosed him as having testicular cancer. The outlook was bleak, as it was thought his career might be in jeopardy. But the surgeons operated, the tumour was found not to be malignant, and he was able to return. So these problems had now been overcome. He had all the attributes that could make him a great player even in the very short term, and in reality these were the players we needed to concentrate on. It is the same argument we had made when going after Petr Cech. We needed players with potential, but who had to demonstrate their worth playing with a big club like Chelsea. The arrival of Robben would give us an alternative to Damien Duff on the left, and allow us to use the Irishman in other positions where, time and again, he had already proven he could be of key importance to us.

In fact, it was precisely to check out the condition of my star Irish international that I went down to Aldershot the next day to watch the reserves playing against West Ham. I would have liked to go and watch our youth and reserve teams more often, but with all the commitments we had, it really was a problem. I had given the first team a few days off, but Duff had continued to work with Mick McGiven and the reserves to see how his Achilles tendon was progressing, and there could be no better test than that of a game. The player, McGiven and the medical staff had all given me ample assurances, but before including him in the squad for the next away fixture, much less playing him, I wanted to see him on the park against meaningful opposition. And I came away convinced of his recovery.

A weekend of FA Cup fixtures reminded us that unfortunately we were already out of the competition, but the enforced break could only do us good and help recharge the batteries for our next vital European tie. That same

Saturday in fact, while some of my fellow coaches would be shouting themselves hoarse from the touchline and dreaming of the Millennium Stadium, I went along to the Sky television studios with Angelo Antenucci, my trusty number 2, to 'spy' on our opponents Stuttgart, who were away to Borussia Dortmund. Scouting is always best done on the spot, obviously, and close to the pitch, but on this occasion the available flight times would have made it all rather complicated. To be sure of arriving back in London in time for training, I would have had to come away after the first half, and so, when the chance to watch a live broadcast of the match presented itself, I snapped it up. After all, it was simply a question of going over what we had already learned about our opponents, like the final revision before an important exam. But I wanted to see them playing an away game, given that we would be the home side on Tuesday, to see what kind of approach they might have. They beat Dortmund 2–0, and all in all I did not see this as a bad sign, as it would warn the boys against dropping their guard unconsciously, following our win in the away leg. Stuttgart are a solid team and I knew they would make life difficult for us. But now we were looking at a huge and important chance for success, and I could not even think about losing.

Chelsea v VfB Stuttgart, Champions League Round of 16, 2nd Leg, Stamford Bridge, 9 March 2004

I decided to start with a 4–5–1 formation, wanting to minimize the risks while exploiting the speed of my wingers and their ability to make threatening runs. Crespo would be the lone striker, but I also wanted Gronkjaer on the right and Duff on the left to lend him a hand. Already in the first half though, I had to change more or less everything around, as with less than half an hour on the clock, Glen Johnson twisted his ankle quite badly and had to come off. I replaced him with Desailly, putting Gallas on the right. I also had to make a tactical change as I saw that during the first 40 minutes, while not actually giving us too many problems, Stuttgart were having rather too much of the initiative, which meant that my 4–5–1 formation – intended initially as a cautionary measure and to limit their options on the flanks – might turn out to be counterproductive in the long term. So I reverted to 4–4–2, simply bringing Gronkjaer further forward and putting Parker out wider on the right of midfield. It was not a great match, I know, but in much the same situation as we found ourselves against Sparta Prague at Stamford Bridge, the result was the important thing, and we duly delivered. There was the odd chance toward the end, but nothing much to speak of other than a near miss one minute from time when, after good work from Crespo and Gronkjaer, the Dane hit the post. It had been bitterly cold out on the pitch, but the atmosphere in the dressing room afterwards was very warm. True, we had won nothing – not even our home leg on this occasion – but we were progressing, and there was a feeling inside that we could go further. Much further.

For this to happen we would have to work hard, play as we knew we could, and enjoy that crucial slice of luck everyone needs. And it was luck that promptly deserted us just two days later, even before we had found out who our next opponents would be, when Cudicini picked up another injury. Diving in the course of the routine practice game that ends our morning training session, he fell badly on his left hand and we soon saw that it might be something serious. We took him along to the hospital for an X-ray, but sadly I had realized straight away that it was not going to be a minor inconvenience. To complicate matters, Sullivan was also sidelined, having strained a thigh muscle in the last reserves game, and so we had only Ambrosio as the one fit first-team goalkeeper.

Champions League Quarter-Final Draw, 12 March 2004

This was the day the draw would be made for the Champions League quarter-finals, and if success in Europe had by now become the main target of our season, my place was still on the training ground. No thought whatsoever of going to Nyon. I have to say that I gave a passing thought more than once to that hand dipping into the basket, but I could do no more than train my team in the best way possible and simply wait for Gary Staker to bring me the news. 'Arsenal!' he exclaimed, walking

200

towards me in the dressing room. For a moment I thought he was joking, but soon enough he had assured me it was true. If it were not for the fear of looking more like a fortune-teller than a manager, seeing what had happened earlier with Lazio, I would claim to have predicted it. But what were we supposed to do? It seemed we were fated this year! It was not the best draw we could have hoped for, but it was all fine by me. I had a team equipped to win, and there was no need to hide from any opposition. We had lost all our games with them this season, and I had never beaten them as a coach. Not that a Champions League quarter-final needed it, but there would be that little extra motivation . . . I like it when there is something at stake, and hoped my players would see it the same way. Arsenal were not unbeatable.

But there were other things to think about, and that evening we set off for Bolton, unfortunately with a big goalkeeper crisis to manage. Cudicini's hand was indeed broken, and I knew that we would have to do without him for three or four weeks at best. No Bolton for him, and more especially no Arsenal. This meant that the time had come for Ambrosio to make his Premiership debut. He was no longer a boy, and this ought to help him through the emotional aspect of such an important first appearance, but it would be equally important for all of us to help him, so that he would be able to show the qualities we selected him for during the summer. As cover, we drafted in the young and athletic Frenchman Makubu-Ma Kalambay, hurriedly giving him a shirt number, 50. He had been training with our goalkeeping coach Giorgio Pellizzaro, and this provided me with a solid guarantee in terms of preparation.

Giorgio has been a friend of mine for many years and we were players together at Catanzaro, but in our association, friendship dictates only when we go out to dinner now and again. The most important thing in a professional relationship is trust, and I am firmly convinced he is probably the best in the world at his particular job. Obviously I cannot pretend to know all the goalkeeping coaches working in different leagues, but I look at the results Giorgio has delivered in the time he has been working with me, and they are undeniably first rate. There is no goalkeeper that has worked with him and not made demonstrable progress. At Fiorentina he took on a big young fellow from the Veneto region. Strapping physique, but a little raw and very inexperienced. Today that same young man, Francesco Toldo, plays for Inter, having been the hero of Italy's Euro 2000 campaign in Holland when they finished the tournament as runners-up, and latterly still runs Gigi Buffon a close second for a national first-team place. At Valencia in Spain, Santiago Canizares was considered little more than a Real Madrid cast-off, yet with Giorgio's help he too ended up playing for his country. As for Cudicini, the improvements in his game have unquestionably been there for all to see, and it was only an odd selection policy on the part of Giovanni Trapattoni that prevented him from claiming a permanent place in the national side, although he did receive a call-up for one friendly game. Giorgio himself was a good goalkeeper, though never a medal winner. In reality he had just the one season in Serie A as a first-choice goalkeeper, and then only because I was there as team captain to organize his defence for him! Joking apart though, it is wonderful to see a goalie of the old school like him, always with the willingness and the ability to keep abreast of new ideas and methods. The Italian goalkeeping tradition is a long one, and the best in the world, but since we have been working in other countries Giorgio has always made a point of looking at how others train and what kind of work they are used to doing, so as to increase his specialist knowledge wherever possible. I trust his assessment of goalkeepers to the point that when I have had to go out and buy one, his opinion has always influenced my final decision. In personal relationships he is forthright, and to people who do not know him he may seem almost to be aggressive in the way he speaks, but this is only because he happens to be shy by nature. Giorgio is the nicest of individuals, and like all my staff, it should be said, fundamentally a partner in everything that teams under my professional guidance have managed to achieve.

Bolton v Chelsea, Reebok Stadium, 13 March 2004

We won, and at this stage the result was the important thing, though I was not altogether happy. Marco Ambrosio did well. Making a Premier League debut is no easy task, especially away from home, and not only did he acquit himself well, he actually got us out of trouble on a couple of occasions. But in the first half we dithered too much. The defence were under pressure, and we were not threading the ball through the midfield as we would normally do. No question about it, we were going through a difficult patch and could only produce so much. Well aware of the situation, I made a point of going into the dressing room and congratulating everyone because I knew we had little else in reserve, and it was a worry, but at the same time they had shown me genuine character. In the final 15 minutes the game was decided by Terry – always there when it matters – and Duff, from an assist by Hasselbaink. After all Damien had been through, I knew the goal meant a lot to him, and I must say I celebrated for him with particular gusto. Getting a player back to fitness in purely medical terms is obviously important, but the process cannot and indeed must never be considered complete until things are back to normal on the pitch and the individual turns in a performance of real significance. So, after his goal at the Reebok Stadium, Damien really could be considered back to normal, and for us this was no small advantage.

Early the following week Carlo Cudicini went to Paris to see a French specialist, but there was nothing else for it: the hand required surgery, and the operation was performed the next day.

Ambrosio had shown me the previous Saturday that he had the ability to play in goal for Chelsea, and he would continue there until Carlo was ready to return, but I do not think I am disrespecting him if I say that this latest injury was a worry. It had not been Cudicini's best season for a number of reasons, but he was still one of the best goalkeepers in Europe and I was bound to wonder what psychological effect his absence might have on the rest of the defence.

In the meantime, the newspapers that week were touting the name of Ottmar Hitzfeld as my possible replacement at Stamford Bridge. The whole business was amusing me by now. I was neither angry nor offended. It seemed to me that the situation must be so obvious to everyone at this point, it was small wonder if people were joining in and having their say. Whilst the directors of the club had seemingly not come out and refused to declare their full confidence in me, they had nonetheless declared their intention to look elsewhere. I might not understand why, given the results we had been achieving and the relationships being created on all levels, and yet it was their prerogative. The press for their part would obviously pick up the scent and unleash their creative flair, suggesting names or following trails uncovered by the usual 'well-informed' subjects. My response may have been a surprise to some people, but it was a matter of indifference to me that the club should talk to Sven-Goran Eriksson or Fabio Capello. And if more names were to pop up, like that of Hitzfeld most recently, it would change absolutely nothing. I was calm and relaxed in a dressing room where I was appreciated, surrounded by highly dedicated professionals, all of us concentrating on the one objective we could set ourselves: winning.

Chelsea v Fulham, Stamford Bridge, 20 March 2004

A very difficult game this one, with all derbies being tricky anyway, and this one more so than any other for obvious reasons of geography. Difficult also in view of the situation illustrated at Bolton, where we had managed to win despite being somewhat below par, having realized that the only way to get back into form was to keep on playing. We had a hugely important game coming up in four days' time: the first leg of a Champions League quarter-final tie against Arsenal, and I felt certain that the outcome of that match would be influenced by the result of this one. A result that could have some small impact in the minds of the fans as well. The Chelsea fans are really marvellous – especially good to me, it must be said, and perhaps I would never thank them enough – and they could be guaranteed to support us come what may, but if we were to give them a little added assurance it would be a good thing for everyone. One win leads to another, and we had to make sure we turned up on Wednesday to meet Wenger and his men with a win against Fulham already under our belts. Selections were more or less dictated by events, as Johnson would be out with an ankle injury for at least as long as Cudicini, which meant Gallas on the right, Desailly and JT the central pair of the back four, and a diamond in midfield with Geremi at the base and Lampard forward playing off the two strikers: Crespo and Gudjohnsen in this instance, as Hasselbaink was also unavailable with a muscle strain. Fulham on the other hand had taken on a completely different look since the departure of Jean Tigana. Under him the team naturally had a more French feel about it, and the football was a touch more spectacular. Since Chris Coleman took over they had played almost always with a lone striker, even at home, going for speed and attacking from the flanks, with Steed Malbranque on the right and Luis Boa Morte on the left. I have to admit that both systems had been equally effective, and they were dangerous opponents for us. I very much admired the job done by Tigana and his invaluable assistant Christian Damiano, and never understood why the situation had to change, although I did read that relationships between the coach and the owner had been soured somewhat by events off the field. But full credit must also go to Coleman for what he has done since. As one would expect from a good former defender, he introduced a more practical approach, but more remarkably, for one so young and with so little experience in top-flight management, he has shown a level of personality and ability that will enable him to go far in this profession. Fulham had recently agreed an extension to his contract, so I read, and it was genuinely deserved.

We scored almost immediately through Gudjohnsen. And what a goal! A cracking drive from 25 yards out into the top corner. The early strike injected us with a welcome shot of confidence and we began to play better, almost doubling our advantage on a couple of occasions. But, as often happens on these occasions when chances are not converted, there is a price to pay, and a quarter of an hour later, a Mark Pembridge free-kick from outside the area took a deflection off the wall and beat Ambrosio, who could do nothing about it. I may not have realized it at that moment, but precisely for the reasons mentioned previously, my team was forced to react. To retake the initiative in a match they had been winning and controlling comfortably. This was a challenge that might produce a really meaningful response. And so it did. I switched the two wide midfielders, Gronkjaer and Duff, but it was not this that changed the game. It was the heart and determination of a team that wanted to win the match. After conceding from the free-kick, Ambrosio really never had to make anything resembling a save, because we allowed Fulham nothing for the rest of the game. Better still, even after Duff had scored the winner, for the second time in as many games, we kept on producing plenty of attacking play. In the second half I made another change to the midfield, putting on Parker for Gronkjaer. This gave a new look to the diamond, with Parker in the anchor role, Lampard on the right, Geremi wide on the left and Duff behind the two strikers. I am not called the Tinkerman for nothing!

I was really pleased at the end. It had not been our most spectacular game or our most resounding victory, but it was perhaps one of the more important ones. Duff on the scoresheet again and fully back to fitness, a psychological success of great importance for the title race, and plenty of momentum to carry us forward with our assault on Europe. Europe in this case being Arsenal, yet again. I read that Arsène Wenger saw a Champions League tie between clubs from the same city as lacking a certain amount of atmosphere and glamour. Well, I suspect that at the moment of the draw he would have been more than happy to be paired with Chelsea. He knows us well, he avoids an away trip, and on the basis of recent results, he can only be confident and optimistic. He and his team would be confident of winning, and who could blame them? But I had a firm belief in my players, and even if the Gunners were effectively the favourites, we had a chance to prove otherwise, and this was enough for me.

Chelsea v Arsenal, Champions League Quarter-Final, 1st Leg, Stamford Bridge, 24 March 2004

I never feel pressure on the eve of a big match, and neither did I used to in my playing days. In fact these occasions fire me up. I feel they bring out the best in me. I knew it was not the same for all my players, but as I walked into my dressing room on the night, I was happy to give myself the illusion that they all felt the same. Then, a little later, as Roberto Sassi was doing our warm-up, I had a quick glance over at the other half of the pitch where the Arsenal players were doing the same.

Thinking about it dispassionately, finding the Gunners in our path at every turn really did seem like a curse. I asked myself, could there be a real reason, an explanation why we never beat them? There are two possibilities. First, it will happen in football that there are these periods when one team never manages to get the better of another. Technically and tactically, in all honesty they were stronger than us. Regardless of what was happening this year, Wenger had been at Highbury since 1996 and had time to build a team. He had allowed the time necessary for Henry, Vieira and Pires to settle, and then to show and express their full worth. Second, there was an *ésprit de corps* in the Arsenal camp that we could not hope to have, for several reasons. For several years now they had become used to fighting for the title, and attempting at least to reach the final stages of the Champions League. And this meant a completely different mentality. From the time I joined Chelsea in 2000, we never had the financial resources that would allow us to build a team step by step. Now, everyone was looking at the Blues and thinking I was the luckiest man on Earth. Someone who could spend wherever and however much he wanted on the transfer market. But no-one remembers that up until last season we did not have so much as one pound to spend on any market. Not even the fruit and vegetable market, never mind the transfer market! This was the great difference between us and Arsenal. This year, we had been given money to spend by Roman Abramovich, and I hope we used it wisely. I had persisted in my philosophy – mentioned more than once on these pages – of buying young players with potential champion pedigree, looking to put together a group, forge a common spirit and encourage growth. Something Arsenal had been doing already for many years. They already had a history, with wins and defeats to their name. Highs and lows, all contributing in whatever way to get them to where they are today. We were still growing. I say it again, Arsenal in March 2004 were genuinely a better team than we were, able to play with an assuredness we could not have, precisely because of our different past history, but now we were taking them on in a Champions League tie, and on this wonderful evening things could change. Maybe not everything, but a good deal.

As it happened our fortunes were changing, and for the better. We were still not the attractive side we had been before Christmas. We had been through some sticky patches with injuries to key players, and this affected the group as a whole. But now we were back on an upward curve. We were improving again: physically, without a doubt; in pure footballing terms, still a little up and down. Arsenal on the other hand were flying, it seemed to me. Everything they attempted, they accomplished. Even when under pressure they managed to keep winning, and this is typical of a successful run.

At the press conference the day before the game, I was asked if after so many disappointments against Arsenal I might have decided to make any radical changes. I always try and field a team that will give me a chance to win the match. I always have done. This is the way I do things and I will never change it. I try to understand how my team is doing at any given time, and help as best I can. On this occasion, seeing how the players had responded recently, I had a number of options and I could only hope to have picked the right one.

I thought a long time before selecting the formation, and in the end went for an 'English' line-up with what might be called a continental attack. In other words, a 4–4–2 with the midfield in line and Gudjohnsen and Mutu the front two. The doubt as to who should play alongside Eidur was one I carried around with me for some considerable time, deciding ultimately on the Romanian the night before. The reason: his footballing qualities and the ability to compete against a team that plays football like the Gunners. Honestly though, I have to say that by the end of the game I was disappointed with his contribution. He had not given me anything remotely near what I was hoping for. On the right of midfield I went for Parker and the greater security I felt he could give me, with Gronkjaer ready to come off the bench should the game need an injection of pace later on. In defence, I had Gallas on the right rather than Melchiot, as he was faster and more of a natural defender – important, as he would certainly be dealing with Robert Pires, a player who tends to drift out wide in the same way that Thierry Henry also does. This move was undoubtedly a success. Henry probably did not have one of his better evenings, but we kept him reined in magnificently.

The match reached an incredible level of intensity, and was a particularly tactical affair. We knew that Jens Lehmann was prone to error, so I had encouraged the boys to put pressure on him, especially when he had the ball at his feet. It was from just such a situation as this that our goal came. Gudjohnsen took his chance especially well, albeit the German goalkeeper did help him a little and in reality was a little unlucky. I do not believe I had ever heard a roar at Stamford Bridge like the one that went up, or perhaps it was simply the joy on my part that made it seem so loud. It really was an extraordinary moment. In the eight minutes that followed we played some fabulous football and could have killed off the game. Rarely had we played so well, and against such fine opposition. But Arsenal are a great team by virtue of their ability to lift themselves stylishly out of situations like this, and it was they who found the net. A splendid goal, alas. A header by Pires, and phenomenal for a player who they tell me had never scored with his head. There was a lot of determination in that equalizer, but on our part there was a measure of naivety too. Pires had made ground magnificently through the middle into the final third, but Lampard, who was on hand, should have put him off balance just sufficiently to ensure he would never even have been in a position to make the header. Certainly a defender who has played in Italy would be expert in tricks of this kind, but Frank is a quality player, and I am sure he will pick them up in time.

In the end it was the right result, even if I was left with the feeling that we had played better, and with the regret of not having made the most of our best moment after taking the lead. Back in the dressing room, I said to the players, 'This result leaves the tie wide open, and with the way we blunted their main attacking weapons, no-one – especially us – must think that there's still a gap that makes them invincible. We'll go and get a result at Highbury.' Words of encouragement for the team, certainly, but I truly believed it possible after a performance that had given me real satisfaction, and suggested there could be more to come. In addition, Arsenal did not appear to be 100% fit, but against a team full of champion footballers like theirs and especially with the return leg two weeks away, observations like this are best left aside.

Before plunging back into Premier League action, we finally welcomed Seba Veron back to the training ground. He had last played a game in England on 9 November, before back problems had forced him to undergo surgery and then a lengthy rehabilitation in Argentina. As a professional footballer, he was perfectly entitled in my estimation to go to a surgeon of his choice – especially for such a delicate operation – naturally with the agreement of the club's own medical staff. The same goes for the post-operative part, broadly speaking, although I felt he could perhaps have returned a few weeks earlier, out of respect for his fellow players. He was well received on the field at Harlington, albeit with a bit of leg-pulling from John Terry, but this was to give all the rest of us a laugh. Veron had in fact returned in surprisingly good condition, just to underline his conscientiousness. Evidently he had followed his recovery programme through to good effect. Not that he was already fit to play, but he was almost there, and with the end of such an important season in sight, his class and the possibility of bringing his experience into play at some key moment could turn out to be crucial.

Maybe it would have been better if he had done his rehab here, so as to stay with the rest of the players, but our facilities, not to put too fine a point on it, were in the process of being improved. This in fact was one of the main topics I had raised with the new owner, regarding plans for the future. A club of this stature could not make do with amateurish facilities. Mr Abramovich understood this straight away when he met the team back in July. It was too important a matter simply to talk about. Things needed to be done. And he did them. If we wanted to operate on the same level as teams like Arsenal and Manchester United, to name just two examples in the English league, we had to start from basic principles. At some point there would be a decision on whether to move the training ground to another location altogether, but in the meantime, works were put in hand at Harlington. The dressing rooms were renovated, and this was among the priorities from a psychological standpoint, as winning teams emerge when a group is able to bond. Our team spirit had always been good, I must say, but we could not have a good situation with a cluster of five small locker rooms. This inevitably caused divisions. There would be Italian speakers changing in one room, all *Gazzetta dello Sport* and gossip, English in another, French and Dutch in the next. In other words, physical separations which miraculously had never led to cliquish rivalries, thanks to the intelligence, cleanliness and professional conduct of the players, but it was a situation that needed to be put right. Now, there is just the one spacious room and a system of nicely designed lockers, each personalized with a nameplate on the door, where getting changed is a pleasure. And there are new showers, offering more than just a straight choice between freezing cold or scalding hot. The gym was moved and enlarged so that fitness coach Roberto Sassi could work better with the team, and the medical room would also be enlarged to take in part of the old gym. These investments were needed, and Mr Abramovich will never regret having made them; indeed in the long term he will come to see that they are worth points in the championship table.

And there were changes to the medical staff too, or rather, necessary additions. I argued the case, I hope without unduly upsetting people who had been with the club over the years, for bringing in important people who could turn an already excellent medical staff into something even better. I have nothing against Dr Neil Fraser, who is a delightful man and who I think is the best English sports doctor there is, nor against Mike Banks, the club's long-serving chief physiotherapist, but I wanted our staff to benefit from the additional expertise of another great professional, Dr Dino Petrucci, who has worked with several Italian football teams, as well as in rugby and athletics, and been consultant to Schalke 04 in the Bundesliga. And the results are evident, as many players have been restored to fitness earlier than expected thanks to his experience. With him came two physiotherapists, Mauro and Alberto, also Italian, who have made a huge contribution to the conditioning of players before and after every match and every training session. A contribution appreciated not only by the Italian contingent, but equally by true blue English players like Terry and Lampard who have come to realize the importance of top-notch physio care for their muscles.

216

Is that a smile, or a perplexed expression?

April 2004 and a storm is
about to hit Highbury
Tomorrow's one will be
worse. For the Gunners…

Ken Bates: the true picture of
your number one fan. The man
who wanted me at Chelsea and
whom I hold in high regard.

Abramovich and
Kenyon looking
thoughtful. Are
they deciding on
my future?

Scottie Parker, the last great buy. He will be one of Chelsea's heroes, I'm sure of it.

A handshake and a ...Sums up how it was with Mutu.

Training was always fun. And cold too. I look as if I'm about to go on a skiing trip.

And they claim Italians gesticulate a lot. Of course we do!

Carlo Cudicini in full flight – where's the ball? I couldn't count the number of miraculous saves he made.

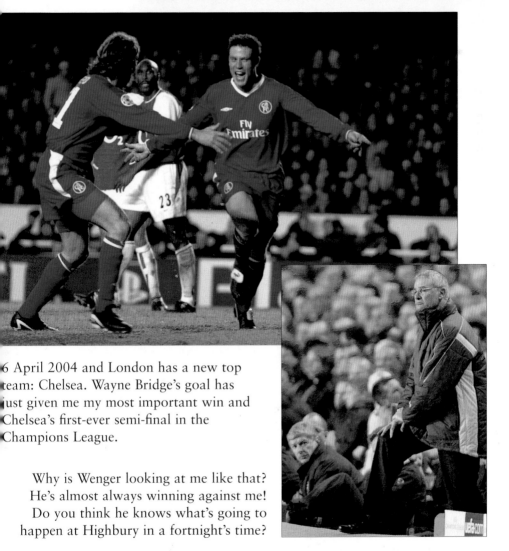

6 April 2004 and London has a new top team: Chelsea. Wayne Bridge's goal has just given me my most important win and Chelsea's first-ever semi-final in the Champions League.

Why is Wenger looking at me like that? He's almost always winning against me! Do you think he knows what's going to happen at Highbury in a fortnight's time?

Previous page:

A bitter disappointment to us all, and Gudjohnsen shows it more than anybody else…

…after lining up in confident mood, we were heartbroken as Morientes' strike takes Monaco into the final…

…and I see my goal slip away.

Farewell day. But it's a good way to go. There are still some pictures of that day that I will never, ever forget.

There is no questioning the professionalism or the practices encountered in the English club system, which I have always openly endorsed and admired, but as Arsène Wenger has shown at Arsenal, blending a variety of different skills and methods can bring benefits. The ability of Mr Abramovich and the management to act on my suggestion showed an appetite for growth on the part of the club, and sent out an extremely positive signal for the future.

Before the training session, I stood Hernan Crespo beside me and gathered the rest of the players around for a few words. 'Hernan is cross with me because I didn't play him in the Champions League game against Arsenal, but the reason I left him on the bench is because you never give him the ball! You don't seem to see him. I'm sure it's nothing personal, but he makes all the right runs, he does the movements the way they should be done, and we've got to exploit the extra opportunities he gives us. This is the reason I bought him. He's one of the world's cleverest and most productive predators in the penalty area, but if we don't play the ball deep to him, what's the use?' The fact that Crespo might or might not be upset with me was unimportant, needless to say. It was all part of a coach's job. Team selections can never keep everyone happy, but the great thing is that they are made in the interests of the team. I spoke about Hernan's situation in front of everybody because it was a problem that needed to be addressed. Patterns of play are not established in a day, and it was quite normal that the team found it easier to pick out Hasselbaink and

Gudjohnsen, as they had been playing together for years, but a top team must exploit all its potential strengths. Playing in blinkers means playing badly. The ability to read different situations is a sign that individuals are learning. All I could do was explain, point out mistakes and continue to try things out – all in training – but there had to be greater tactical awareness on the part of the players.

Chelsea v Wolves, Stamford Bridge, 27 March 2004

We had to be careful that the bright lights of Europe did not distract us, and I trusted the prospect of a visit by Wolves, an easy fixture on paper, would not cause the team to lose concentration. My own day started off with a fizz right from the early morning. I take little notice of the press and do not read the papers very much, but I always take a look at the *Gazzetta dello Sport* with my breakfast cappuccino, and since becoming more familiar with the language, I try to read at least something from the English sports pages too. On this particular morning I was greeted at breakfast not only by my yoghurt with forest fruits and the habitual coffee, but also by a picture of Sven-Goran Eriksson visiting Peter Kenyon at his apartment, on the front page of one of the tabloids. The situation was made even more comical by the fact that 31 March was my daughter's birthday, and I was planning to give the players Sunday and Monday off, not least to recoup the energy being expended on the cup, as I had decided to go to Rome and celebrate with Claudia over dinner, albeit a couple of days before the event. Leaving the house with a trolley and a bag, I was getting into the car when a photographer popped out at the corner of my street and duly accomplished his paparazzo mission. He could hardly have been more lucky. I just smiled, but I could see the headline next day . . . 'Ranieri packs his bags', or 'Ranieri on his way'! For the readers, I would be the man moving out of Chelsea. In reality I was on the way to the ground to pick up three points against Wolverhampton Wanderers, who would be bringing the strength of desperation and no doubt some solid resistance with them.

I made a few changes from the Arsenal game, using different players out wide both in the back line and in midfield: Babayaro and Melchiot in defence, Joe Cole and Geremi further forward. I knew Makelele and Lampard were tired, but I kept them in to avoid changing the heart of the formation.

'Careful now! We've got to forget about Arsenal because today is a different game altogether, but no less important in terms of our ultimate objectives. They will be determined, and they could well go in hard because it's all on the line for them. What we've got to do, above all, is move the ball around quickly.'

The game started off well as Melchiot found space on the right, and after three minutes we were already in the lead. Then disaster struck. On 22 minutes we allowed them an equalizer following a bad mess-up between Babayaro and Terry, who allowed Camara to pick up a rebound. But it was our attitude that I had problems with. Wolverhampton would have even deserved to go ahead, and in fact at the start of the second half they scored with a header by Jody Craddock from a corner-kick. At that point the fans were magnificent, as they saw we were in difficulty (though strictly speaking we should not have been) and got right behind the team. They continued to chant their support for me and yet again voiced their displeasure at the trumpeted arrival of Eriksson. This kind of affection and esteem touches me inside, but as already mentioned, I find it embarrassing because I am never sure how to respond. But at that moment the only problem I had was how to turn the tide in this particular game and get the result we wanted. I brought on Hasselbaink, who on a special day for statistics, with Frank Lampard notching up 100 consecutive Premier League appearances, decided he too would finally reach another historic milestone of 100 goals in the Premier-ship. It was a dream Jimmy had been chasing since the beginning of the season, and more pressingly for the last six games, during which he had been stuck on 99. And it was deserved. A striker of his stature does not really need the reassurance of numbers, but a total of 100 goals in the Premiership alone is so important, and certainly the crowning achievement in a great career. I could never play him as often as he would have liked – every game, in other words – but he knows perfectly how much I value him. I had already been his coach at Atletico Madrid and I knew all about him, positive and negative aspects alike. Jimbo is a grumbler but a model professional with an uncommonly sharp eye for goal. He may not possess the supreme footballing qualities of other great players in the history of the game but just having him in the penalty area can guarantee success in certain circumstances. And this year he was really on form, in great physical shape and wonderfully motivated. The results were there for all to see.

At all events he won the Wolves match for us. Not content with knocking in his 100th goal, he went on to celebrate with a hat-trick. The final scoreline of 5–2, to be truthful, was a heavier defeat than Dave Jones's team deserved.

I learned after the game that several newspapers would be running 'stories' next day on how I had already signed with Tottenham for the coming season. It would certainly be the perfect way to use those photos taken outside my home earlier in the day. 'Ranieri moves to White Hart Lane . . .' Coincidentally, our next Premier League fixture would be with Spurs. Of course I had experience of these things, and I knew the journalists would have quizzed me about this and about the photograph of Eriksson's visit to Kenyon's home rather than asking questions about the match, so I decided not to attend the post-match press conference. No disrespect to anyone, but what could I say? Untrue – I had not even spoken to Spurs, much less signed any contract with them? That it was hardly important to me who Sven chose to take an aperitif with? Would they believe me, or would whatever I said end up being manipulated in some way or other? I would have preferred to talk about the character of my team, how they had managed even on a bad day to put five goals past their opponents. I would have liked to talk about Hasselbaink's hat-trick or the usual supergoal served up by Frank Lampard. And so I decided that the best way to give everyone due respect and above all acknowledge Jimmy's golden moment, on his birthday, would be to send the man himself to talk to the press. He could go and speak to the journalists, and I would go to Rome and help my daughter celebrate her birthday.

Whether or not my decision to miss the press conference had the effect of aborting the false headline of my supposed agreement with Tottenham I could not say, but happily the story did not get into the papers. Just the odd line in the news-in-brief sections: 'Spurs express possible interest in Ranieri'. Even the 'suitcases' photo outside my London home appeared without any sensational caption, thank goodness. One less irritation to endure. That same day, as it happened, Eriksson called a press conference to announce that he had agreed a two-year extension of his contract as England coach. This brought down the curtain on the Eriksson–Chelsea saga.

APRIL

'OK chaps, my fault! This time I got it wrong'

In all my professional life, there had never been a month that looked as potentially decisive as this, both person- ally and competitively. My message to the players and to the press continued to be that the Champions League was nothing more than a beautiful dream and we had to keep our minds on the Premiership. And it was true, but perhaps I was trying to make the point to myself more than anyone, so as to defuse the tension as much as possible ahead of the return leg against Arsenal and, who could say, two legs of a semi-final tie to follow. Technically and tactically, games like these can be simple enough to manage. Psychologically and emotionally, they are not so simple. This was a new experience for many of us, me included. We could only imagine what it might be like, the romance and the thrill. Yes, maybe I was right: it was just a beautiful dream. But how wonderful to be living it.

Dreams though, are followed by awakenings, and we

223

would need to be wide awake in time for the next match with Tottenham. It may not quite compare to some of the big cross-town rivalries in other parts of Europe, and especially in the Italian league, but the atmosphere when Chelsea play Spurs at White Hart Lane is one of real sporting hostility. The rivalry is palpable, and the fans love it. Happily – in contrast to our dismal record against Arsenal – we had not lost a league fixture at White Hart Lane for many years. It had certainly not happened during my time in SW6, and I was told this particular unbeaten away run went back as far as 1990. Three days later we would be returning to north London for our European clash with the Gunners, and as invariably is the case in these situations, when two important games are played in a short space of time, the second one was the crucial one. Always that doubt: better to rest a few players for the other game and avoid the risk of injuries, or put out the strongest side? The classic dilemma. But there is no rule, no handbook. A coach has to follow his instinct, and my preference was always to field my best team. There is no planning for injuries: they can happen in training and matches alike, and players do not simply fall away. In other words, for a player in top condition – as is the case with all our players – there can be no question of fatigue caused by playing two games in three days. My own preference is to go with the team that looks most likely to win on the day, unless I am looking to try a tactical experiment, or faced with opponents likely to cause me particular problems, which Spurs really did not.

Tottenham v Chelsea, White Hart Lane, 3 April 2004

It could hardly have gone better. We won, we kept a clean sheet, and I had answers to all the questions I was asking. Given the potential hazards lying in wait, there was every good reason to be gratified. This win would be the best possible travelling companion to have on our next European trip. Europe, just along the road from White Hart Lane . . .

First of all, there was another fine performance from Ambrosio, keeping out a shot from Robbie Keane in the first half, and crucially, a header from Anthony Gardner five minutes from time. All credit must be given to our goalkeeper, in view of the way that things had gone in the course of a season that might well have seen him go into something of a slide. With the arrival of Neil Sullivan he had been relegated to an even more marginal role than the one he already knew was all he could expect: number two to Cudicini. There was no pecking order as such between Marco and the Scot, though it is true that when Carlo was injured the first time, I had given Sullivan the nod precisely because of his greater experience in the English game. To be fair, new surroundings, limited first-team opportunities and the birth of a lovely little daughter might well have distracted and even demotivated him. Instead he responded positively, and with the wheel of fortune giving him his chance, he had taken it with both hands. It would be unfair to say he astonished us all, as it was on the strength of his abilities that he had been brought to Chelsea in the first place, but he did surprise everyone a little nonetheless. Hats off to him for his performances and the way he had handled himself in such a delicate situation. In reality the job of a reserve goalkeeper can be more tricky than others, as he may be thrown in the deep end at any given moment but is still expected not to let anyone down. Once again, here at White Hart Lane, he was a big performer.

The game was won for us with a first-half goal by a 'red hot' Hasselbaink, but what reassured me most of all, with the Gunners clash coming up, was the ability of the team to stay in the game. To control the opposition. Statistically, after all, we had had practically the same number of chances as Spurs, but even as the away side it was clear that we had taken the game to them and dictated the tempo. Returning to the dressing rooms, it was confirmed to me that Arsenal had just lost their FA Cup tie against Manchester United at Villa Park, as we were completing our win. This could have been interpreted as a slight boost for us, but then there was also the threat that the Highbury club might simply be more interested in the Champions League. In contrast to what I had decided to do in a similar situation on the same day, Wenger had chosen to keep Henry and Reyes on the bench and give a start to young Jeremie Aliadiere. I say 'similar' rather than identical, as their game happened to be the semi-final of an important competition, the FA Cup. A game of considerably greater significance than a league fixture involving a team quite a few points behind them in the table, it must be said. When a manager leaves the best player in his team either on the bench or up in the stand, he automatically sends out a message to the rest of his staff: the game is important, up to a certain point . . . I did not see the Villa Park game, but leaving aside the pride factor, I suspected the Arsenal players must unconsciously have put this interpretation on the game, and so I did not want to fool myself into thinking the cup exit could be some sort of alarm bell for them. Indeed the impact on us could be distinctly negative.

Back on the team bus, I took a close look at the match statistics and noted one or two interesting items. The clean sheet we had managed against Tottenham was our 28th of the season – another record equalled. And the 1–0 scoreline was the 13th of the season, a number that was also a record for Chelsea. Not a hugely significant statistic, but surely 1–0 has a kind of resonance, especially at Highbury? The fact that we were going there as experts at defending a 1–0 lead, as the Gunners had been so famously in the past? It was just a passing thought, but one that showed yet again how much I was looking forward to this tie, and I was certain my players would be just as focused and conscientious in their approach.

Back at our training ground I was presented with the Barclaycard Premiership Manager of the Month award for the second time in the season, and again I received it with enormous pride. Pride strictly untinged by other sentiments. I was asked by one or two journalists if this might not be seen as a kind of slap in the face for whoever was seeking to replace me as head coach of Chelsea. I can promise that the notion had never even occurred to me. As far as I was concerned, it was a job well done by everyone and executed on the pitch by the players. I felt more like a representative collecting a prize on behalf of everyone involved. I may have thought about the fact that no manager in the history of Chelsea had ever won the award, certainly, but not about my contract or my future. People might not believe it, but I really did understand the mentality of Roman Abramovich. I knew he would make his decisions independently of these factors, and maybe even regardless of whatever we might achieve by the end of the season. My only real regret is that they had presented me with the award almost secretly, at Harlington, whereas I had seen that many of my colleagues and other players had their presentations at the stadium, before a home game. My programme notes always ended with the words 'Together with all our hearts,' and in this spirit I would like to have shared the award with everyone, because it was won by all of us, working together. Fans, players, and technical staff. It would have been better done at Stamford Bridge. All the same, I stood the little trophy on my mantelpiece, ready for the next trip to Rome, and turned my attention entirely to the match with Arsenal.

Strangely enough, for such an important game, there was not a great deal of preparation to do, either tactically or physically. All we did at Harlington was run through a session or two to loosen the muscles and try out a couple of tactical moves, but I had in any case decided on an overnight stop. It seemed a little comical as I handed our team manager Gary Staker a notice to pin up on the board at the training ground, reminding the players to bring their passports, given that we were only going a few miles across London. But Uefa regulations require it, and so it was a case of everyone on the tube with their passports. Well, not actually on the Underground of course, although it would certainly have taken us there. We were perfectly familiar with the stadium, the pitch and the dressing rooms, but we still went along to Highbury on the evening before the game. I wanted Ambrosio to get a good look at the lights and the balls. Even the smallest details can be crucial at this level, and the question of footballs was actually not such a minor detail. In cup games, especially, Arsenal had been playing for some months with balls provided by their sponsor, which naturally were FIFA approved, but different to the ones we were using. The new balls were much the same as those that would be used for Euro 2004. They were lighter, and tended more to change direction in flight. Even the pattern printed on the surface, character-ized by what look like elliptical bands, could have the effect of confusing a goalkeeper unfamiliar with it. I had asked for two or three to be brought down to Harlington so that our goalkeepers could begin getting used to them beforehand, but it still seemed a good idea to go and try them out directly in Arsenal's own backyard. Training at Highbury on the eve of the game would also give me the chance, should it even be necessary, to focus the minds of the players on the fact that this was a European tie. An appointment with destiny. Appointment with a capital 'A'.

We had played them so many times, I had seen them and talked about them so many times, and I had every respect for them. I knew we had not beaten them in 17 games, although this number needed careful analysis. At some time in the future it might look as if Chelsea had been regularly outclassed by Arsenal over a number of years, but those of us who were involved in these games know very well that there was never such a big gap between the sides. They had always been fiercely contested matches and on some occasions we were genuinely unlucky. They had won games that we would have deserved at least to draw, and drawn games that we could reasonably have won. But the history of football is not a matter of theory. Success and failure are not determined by points, as in boxing, diving or gymnastics; they are measured by results. All the same, I had never felt 'beaten' by Arsenal, and this was still the way I saw it even now. I remember once saying to Abramovich, 'Roman, I don't know when we'll ever manage to beat Arsenal, but I sense that when we finally do, it will be on a very important occasion!' And what more important occasion than the chance of a place in the Champions League semi-final? These were my very thoughts when all of a sudden, during our evening training session, the pitch was inundated by a huge cloudburst. An event like this would no doubt be interpreted as a bad omen by some of my more superstitious colleagues, but not even this could have shaken my belief. I went to sleep in the certain knowledge that we would make a game of it next day, and with no doubts about the formation I had decided on some days earlier.

The team was the same one that had beaten Tottenham on Saturday, and this selection must have surprised the newspapers rather, as nearly all of them had published their probable formations on match day assuming that Crespo would start in attack. I had decided to go into the game – the most important of my career to date – with the team that gave me the best chance of winning, which meant that the two strikers at the front had to be Jimbo and Eidur, because of the understanding they had with one another, their current form, and the way they both managed to combine talent and practicality. The game might evolve in such a way that we had to think about using Crespo, and I was happy to have him available, but the selection of the starting line-up was firmly decided.

I was not surprised in the slightest by the 'miraculous' recovery of the three Arsenal players, Ljungberg, Cole and Reyes, who Wenger had said might be out for several weeks, and perhaps a month in at least one case. Time spent coaching in Naples had taught me how to read the three-card trick. I was perhaps less sure of whether Arsène would start with Reyes or with Bergkamp, but that Jose Antonio Reyes was available to him there could be no doubt.

Arsenal v Chelsea, Champions League Quarter-Final, 2nd Leg, Highbury, 6 April 2004

We were up bright and early, though not because of being overly tense or unsettled by the occasion. It was simply that the hotel made a mistake and called us all one hour too soon. But what was done was done, and there was no point in getting upset. Better to save all our energies for the stadium.

As we drove into Highbury I was watching my players closely. Everything was calm. I am always very careful to try and gauge the mood in the dressing room before a game. I knew the boys well by that time, and I could see they were focused, but relaxed. I sensed they were not at all worried, even in the face of such a big undertaking. There was no hint of them being burdened by the weight of those 17 winless games against the Gunners. Only a determination to break the duck. Seeing them with this attitude set my mind even more at rest. It reinforced the conviction, the certainty I had, that we would be able to take our chances without holding back – not necessarily that we would win the game, though in my heart I hoped we would. Even my pre-match pep-talk was a fairly straightforward task, but I wanted to convey all the determination that has always been my career trademark, because I was already beginning to live this game for real, as if I had been out on the pitch as a player.

'Now listen chaps, we've got nothing to lose, and this is a weapon we've got to use in our favour. They're the favourites. Big club. But they have to win at all costs. We can do something really good here, so let's start laying the foundations for our success right here, tonight!'

It was a positive mindset, and there was no wavering even when we came unstuck in first-half injury-time. We were back into the dressing room at half-time behind to a Reyes goal. In reality they had produced no more than one or two bursts of any significance and we were comfortably in the game, although at that point there could be no more slip-ups. Shipping a goal in injury-time is psychologically one of the worst things that can happen, even if only at the end of the first half, but my team were tough in the psychological department. That goal by Reyes could have slaughtered us, but it was not going to.

I made one change at the interval, putting on Gronkjaer in place of Parker. Scottie had done nothing wrong at all. In fact he had shown determination and discipline, as ever, but I needed the pace of Jesper to keep Ashley Cole busy by forcing him to defend and pinning him back in his own half. This was important, remembering what I have already said about Cole: that in my opinion he is one of Arsenal's main attacking weapons.

In that second half, we dominated. It was a sustained assault, delivered with an air of real superiority. We whipped up the pace, whereas they were a spent force. I had never seen Arsenal in such physical difficulty, but this was very much our doing. There was evidently something magic in the air for us that night, so much so that the equalizer came from a long-range effort by Makelele, no less. Claude would hardly ever shoot at goal, although

233

I had always urged him to try his luck. Whether Lehmann may have been unsighted at the moment the ball came towards him I cannot say, but he undeniably gave further ammunition to his critics by attempting a parry that ended up, fortunately for us, looking rather like a bungled volleyball forearm pass. The German had disregarded the most basic of goalkeeping rules. Instead of diverting the ball away, he had stopped it right in the middle of the penalty area. At that moment I was too happy to worry about Lehmann's personal tragedy which, to be frank, was really no problem of mine. The fact is that Lampard pounced on the loose ball, exploiting the situation to the full, and despatched it greedily – angrily almost – into the net. Among his other considerable qualities, Frank has one that cannot be taught: a predatory instinct that ensures he is always in the right place at the right moment to take advantage of sharp chances. He is almost unique in this.

From that moment Arsenal were unable to respond. They had the skill, obviously, but not the strength. I saw that the tie was ours for the taking, but we had to finish it off, although even had it gone to extra-time I really do not know how the Gunners would have managed. I brought on Joe Cole, knowing he could give me more thrust than a tired Duff. Tired, because at half-time in Saturday's game against Spurs I had told him he would be coming off after five or ten minutes, but he had then upped his game and so I let him play the full ninety. In any event Damien had given me a solid performance here at Highbury too, with a very disciplined exhibition of covering play. The whole team was playing exceptionally well, with great performances from Makelele and Gudjohnsen, and though Jimbo had not managed to find the net, his contribution on a competitive level had been fundamental.

Wenger's men were on the ropes, and at five minutes from time appeared to be on the point of capitulating. After a blistering run down the left, Joe Cole found Gudjohnsen in the middle of the area, and it was only through a miracle goal-line clearance by Ashley Cole that his finish was kept out. I also took off Hasselbaink and put on Crespo, as I wanted a specialist striker with fresh legs in the area. Knowing that Hernan was angry with me for not including him in the starting line-up, I now wanted to put his anger to good use in some way. Turn it into something positive. In the end there was no need, as just one minute after Cole's last-ditch heroics, Wayne Bridge stepped up to score the most important goal of his career, and the career of many others on our side. A goal that made Chelsea history, or at least rewrote the chapter telling of the club's involvement in European competitions. A beautifully worked one-two on the left with Gudjohnsen, whose touch on the return pass was silky smooth, and the ball was in the net behind Lehmann – blameless this time. I went crazy. Normally I manage to keep every kind of emotion in check, especially when in the dugout, but this time it was impossible. The surge of pure joy was too strong. I ran onto the pitch yelling, fists clenched and punching the air above my head. I was moved almost to tears and would never be ashamed to say so. It was the most extraordinary moment, the most electric thirty seconds of my entire life in football. We were through to the semi-finals of the Champions League, no doubt about it, and in those final minutes I was able both to enjoy the fantastic result and to regain control of my emotions just a little. And when referee Markus Merk sounded the triple blast on his whistle, it was party time. We had done it. Done it in more ways than one. We had exorcized our Arsenal demon and won the first Champions League quarter-final in the history of Chelsea FC, but perhaps best of all we had come of age, and shown it. That group of champion footballers assembled at the beginning of last summer had been transformed, in the best fairy-tale tradition, and turned into a real team. It was a result as sensational as it had been deserved, and clearly it could not be the end of the story. It had to mark a new start. And it had to be a night we would enjoy to the full and remember always.

The party began straight away in the dressing room, needless to say. Everyone was hugging everyone else, so much so that after all the players had taken their turn, I too found myself embracing Roman Abramovich. It was not a prelude to any kind of 'love affair', as the events of the coming weeks would show, but it was a wonderful moment. We were intoxicated with joy, but I stayed calm and collected enough to face the press, and above all to make a point of not embracing Peter Kenyon. A hand-shake and congratulations would be quite sufficient in his case. After the game, with my mobile all but locking up as the messages poured in, I had occasion to see yet again and to appreciate the gentlemanly conduct of the Gunners. Fierce rivals on the pitch, and equally sporting off it. Many of the Arsenal players came up and congratulated me, notably Freddie Ljungberg who was particularly sincere. Then, as we were leaving, vice-chairman David Dein shook my hand with the words 'You deserve it!' which I will never forget.

They say that when a manager gets all his substitutions exactly right, it means the initial selection must have been wrong. I think all my selections were right on this occasion. Obviously the credit must go to the team for the way they competed, but this time I do believe I made all the right moves. A word of praise must also go to our illustrious fitness advisor, Professor Sassi. The results of his endeavours were clear for all to see in the contrasting physical condition of the two teams that night.

Less welcome on the night, strange as it may seem, was the news that Real Madrid had been knocked out. This meant we would be facing Monaco in the semi-final, whereas I would have preferred Real. The principality had a team that was solid, improving, and showing very good away form too. Real Madrid on the other hand looked to me like a team in some difficulty, and even with all their star players were totally lacking in confidence at the time. Aside from the fact that the prospect of playing at the Bernabeu would have heightened the prestige of the tie from our point of view, I really did think Real would have suited us better. In any event we would think about Monaco in a few days' time. For the moment, we would enjoy this triumph.

But now we had a problem. This euphoria had to be put to one side if we did not want to risk losing our concentration. The danger now was that we would start thinking only about Monaco, and looking at Premier League fixtures simply as days to be counted off. And it would be a mistake twice over to let our determination slip for the odd game, because then it would be difficult to pick up the rhythm again for the important ones. Then there was the fact that, with the Cup success under our belts, I had given more than a passing thought to the notion of catching our rivals in the title race too. I like to think positively, or perhaps I am an incurable optimist, but I was hoping the effect of that result would be critical both for us, with the win providing a springboard for further progress, and for them, with the defeat returning like a boomerang to cut through their confidence.

With this in mind, I was very curious to see how Arsenal would react at the weekend against Liverpool in the first Premiership fixture following their Champions League exit. A tricky one, even if it was a home game, but seeing the way they were able to come back twice from behind and win against the Reds, even after the psychological blow they had been dealt by us, I realized we were never going to catch them. It was a magnificent show of strength and character by them. And at that moment, I think my players also acknowledged subconsciously that Arsenal were going to be deserving winners of the Premiership title, as our thoughts turned more and more to the Champions League.

But we had to keep pace in the title race too, if we

were going to make sure of second place. True, a win like the one at Highbury generates new stimuli and good vibrations, but beating a top team like Arsenal involves an expenditure of nervous energy three times the normal level, and we knew we could pay the price, starting with our next home game against Middlesbrough.

Chelsea v Middlesbrough, Stamford Bridge, 10 April 2004

I tried to change things around, and to find fresh legs by using players like Babayaro, but all to no avail, at least as far as the result was concerned. To tell the truth, I thought it might even have been worse, whereas in fact we created three clear scoring chances, hit the post through Hasselbaink and kept Mark Schwarzer busy for the whole 90 minutes. Another positive was the performance by Veron. I had put him on for the final half-hour precisely to check on his condition, and I could not have been more satisfied. Seeing the effect of his presence and his ability to galvanize the play, I felt that he was more or less back to his best, and this could turn out to be an unexpected bonus in the immediate future. The only concern was a nasty knock received by Claude Makelele as the result of a particularly hard tackle by Mendieta – Gaizka of all people! I thought Claude might have broken something, and for a while I really was worried. He had been shaken up, but fortunately there were no lasting consequences.

One of the first points I was keen to make at the post-match press conference, after paying a deserved tribute to my players, was that we now recognized Arsenal as champions. It is not in my nature to give up, and I would always want my players to have the same attitude, but the way things were this weekend we had to take stock of the new reality. They could not be caught: our aim now was to secure second place, and nothing less would do as far as I was concerned.

As a Catholic, Easter is an important feast for me and one I would always want to observe, but I had become accustomed by now to the rigours and the pace of the English season, with its calendar crammed full of fixtures, especially on and around public holidays. So, not too much time for Easter eggs and the traditional Italian *colomba* cake. Instead, our minds had to be on the next away fixture with Aston Villa up in Birmingham. Never an easy game, and this time it would give me an opportunity to see how my players were reacting after the contrasting events of the previous week. The first leg of the Monaco tie was eight days away, with another Premier League fixture against Everton still to be negotiated before then; but it was already very much in our minds, and whatever assessments or observations might be made in the coming days were bound more or less subconsciously to have Monaco as their focal point.

Aston Villa v Chelsea, Villa Park, 12 April 2004

This time I was less angry than on our last trip to Villa Park in November when we went out of the Carling Cup, but it was still another loss. The thing that annoyed me most was that in just two games we had frittered away the advantage so painstakingly built up over Manchester United in the race for second place.

This being the second game in the space of 48 hours, I had to rotate the squad as much as possible, putting Huth in central defence and, since Makelele was out, moving Parker into his preferred central midfield position, with Geremi and Duff on the flanks. In attack, on this occasion, I used the pairing of Crespo and Mutu. The Argentinian had a great game and scored a welcome brace, whereas Mutu was a big disappointment, both in this game and, I have to say, more generally during the entire season. I had expected much more of him: more goals, more team spirit, more pride in the club's colours, and more respect. He was young and full of potential, certainly, but looking towards the future – for his own good – he would have to get himself more organized if he was going to make the most of his promise. I had no interest in finding out whether or not there was any substance in the stories being put about by the newspapers concerning his celebrity lifestyle, but one thing was certain. Unless his attitude was going to be 100% professional, it would be a waste. He had all the skills and flair, but to win championships things have to be right between the ears too.

We started off well, and for the first quarter of an hour there seemed to be only one team in it, and that was Chelsea. In fact we took the lead, but just when it looked as if we could start controlling the game, we were unable to deal with their reaction. From a competitive point of

241

view the team gave it everything, as always. John Terry was involved in a battle royal on high balls with their lofty centre-forward Peter Crouch, and was perhaps our best player, along with Crespo, but we were unable to hold on to the ball. It was a moment of naivety on the part of Mario Melchiot in the area that gave Villa a penalty and lost us the game. I could only hope that these eminently avoidable mistakes would not be repeated in the Champions League semi-final.

The defeat at Villa Park brought us down to Earth with a brutal bump after our night of heroics at Highbury, and perhaps this might be no bad thing.

But winning is a habit, and with the Monaco clash now just around the corner, I was hoping we would be able to put in a good performance against Everton at the weekend and get a result.

Chelsea v Everton, Stamford Bridge, 17 April 2004

It was a splendid late spring day. The first hint of summer as far as the weather was concerned, but in my mind there were already storm clouds gathering even before the game was due to start. I was not able to use Gudjohnsen as he had picked up a dose of flu during the week and was laid up, but when Dr Fraser told me that Damien Duff had been forced to stay in bed with a thermometer and a sore throat for company, I did not take the news at all well.

The outlook that Saturday morning was bleak indeed,

and it must be said that the afternoon turned out little better. Even playing our attacking game and creating a number of chances, we picked up a second goalless draw at home and, worse still with the Champions League tie coming up, I lost William Gallas after twenty minutes with a thigh muscle strain. Monaco could be devastating in attack down the left with Patrice Evrà and especially Jérôme Rothen going forward. The plan, already adopted in the quarter-final against Arsenal, would have been to put Gallas out wide on the right to keep them in check. It had worked to perfection against Henry and Pires, but with these other two Frenchmen it looked as though I would not have the chance to try it again.

I tried everything against Everton in the final fifteen minutes, making substitutions to bring on Gronkjaer and the Portuguese youngster Felipe Oliveira, and changing tactics, but in the end it made no difference. We ran no risks at the back and allowed them nothing, but neither did we score. At last, though, we really could start thinking about the game with Monaco.

On Monday 19 April, the day before the match, we flew out to Monte Carlo where we found a relaxed atmosphere, warm sunshine and a good many of our fans. I had told the players the day before that this was a big and historic match, but for a team like ours it was no more or less than a logical outcome of what we had been doing, and a step along the way to what we were capable of doing. I wanted them to realize the importance of the occasion, but not to choke with the pressure of it. So maximum focus but a relaxed approach. When teams are too tense they can never express themselves, as nerves will get the upper hand.

I had agreed that we should stay in the town centre, but perhaps the choice of hotel was a mistake. It was a magnificent place on the hill leading up to the Casino from St Devote, the first leg of the F1 Grand Prix circuit. Real Madrid had stayed there too for their quarter-final, although it was not a problem of superstition – not my style, as the reader will surely have discovered by now – but rather of logistics. Little chance to cut ourselves off from the general commotion, and a lot of fans were camped outside. There was an unparalleled view of the yachts in the harbour, certainly, but the only view I wanted to see was the final of the Champions League. Standing between us and that final was a high-quality team that had made its way quietly and efficiently through the draw, inflicting an amazing 8–3 victory over Deportivo in the group stage, before finally muscling through and dumping out the *galacticos* of Real Madrid, no less, in the quarter-finals.

I had watched them time and again on video and knew them by now as if they were my own players. And it was for this reason that I feared them. The danger was mainly from the left, as I mentioned, with the Evrà–Rothen combination, but not only from there. The two strikers knew where to position themselves, moving wide so that Bernardi could make his runs from midfield, and more especially to make space for the lightning-fast Ludovic Giuly cutting in from the right. They did not give away

244

much at the back, and between the posts they had Flavio Roma, a worthy exponent of the Italian goalkeeping tradition. In some of their attacking moves they reminded me of Arsenal, even if the characteristics of the main striker in the two teams were slightly different. Monaco had Fernando Morientes, and I admire this forward as much as I am wary of him. In my view he is one of the best strikers in the world, and indeed I would have liked to bring him to Chelsea at the beginning of the season. The complete package, he contributes to the build-up play, shoots with either foot and is deadly with his head. I knew that Didier Deschamps' side was very dangerous on the road, and with this in mind I really wanted to try and take a big step toward booking our place in the final in this first leg.

That evening we familiarized ourselves with the pitch in a training session so stringently regulated by tough UEFA security that even the Argentinian tennis star Guillermo Coria, third in the ATP rankings at the time and playing in the Monte Carlo Masters Series event at the Country Club, was unable to gain entry and shake hands with his idol Hernan Crespo. We tried to make the meeting happen, but there was nothing to be done.

Just as there was nothing to be done, unfortunately, for Duff and Gallas, who would be two sorely missed absentees. But something else happened that evening which troubled me far more. It came to my knowledge that, while we had been preparing for the match, Chelsea had had a meeting with representatives of José Mourinho, manager of FC Porto. I had put up with a lot in these last few months, but this was really hard to take. It showed a lack of respect not just for me but for the players, and for all the effort we were putting in to try and achieve something historic for Chelsea.

Monaco v Chelsea, Champions League Semi-final, 1st Leg,
Louis II Stadium, 20 April 2004

A date and a match I will not easily forget. A defeat that will always come back to haunt me. To tell the story of the encounter, which we had all been so looking forward to, I simply have to start from the end.

I wanted so badly to win this game, but instead we lost, and I was the main culprit. It was a heavy loss too, and although I hoped we might be able to turn it around in the second leg, it would be very difficult. I know perfectly well where and why I made the mistake, but this certainly doesn't make me feel any better about it. With our opponents down to ten men after Zikos was sent off (seen later on TV, a decision that was far from justified), I put on an extra striker and inevitably we lost our shape. I had already thought, mistakenly, that I could inject something different after half-time by bringing on Veron to replace a spent Gronkjaer, but this only made things worse. Jesper had not played well, but Veron was even poorer and did not track back to cover in defence. The memory of his magical half-hour against Middlesbrough had flattered to deceive, as Seba now showed nothing near the quality he paraded on that occasion. I was afraid of Monaco's away form, and once we had the advantage of an extra man I wanted to kill off the tie there and then. But with Crespo, Hasselbaink and Gudjohnsen on the pitch together we were all at sea, and in an attempt to patch up the mistake – having already taken off Melchiot to bring on Jimmy – I substituted Huth for Parker. The debacle was complete. All credit must go to Monaco, not least for their three spectacular goals, all of them difficult chances, but I had given them a helping hand. My players made the odd mistake too, undoubtedly, but I knew full well that the blame was principally mine. What is more, I had let myself be affected by anger over the meeting between the club and Mourinho's agent, and wanted the win as a way of retaliating, proving a point. But it was a mistake. Utmost respect for the opposition, the chance to take advantage of their misfortune and the events of the night before had combined to influence my judgement, and I made the wrong choices. This was the first time such a thing had happened to me. But the fault was all mine. At my age and with my experience I should have been able to rise above situations like this, but in the end it was human nature that determined the outcome.

And speaking of human nature, hats off to Roman Abramovich, who was quick to cheer everyone up in the dressing room and even invited us all onto his yacht to spend a little time together. A splendid gesture, not likely to be made by many club chairmen, and one I very much appreciated even at a moment when I was hurting so much inside. Indeed if anything it made me feel worse, compounding my sense of guilt.

But I am a fighter by nature, and after the inevitable sleepless night I was already working on how to put things right. This time more than at any other, the players would have to help me out. For once it was I who had messed up, and we all had to try and come out of it together. It would be extremely difficult, but it might not be impossible.

When we met up again for training at Harlington two days later, I found the atmosphere understandably subdued. Gathering them all around in the middle of the pitch, I said my piece one more time.

'OK chaps, my fault! This time I got it wrong. I misread the game, and made the wrong changes at the wrong times.'

They listened in silence, heads down.

'But now we've got to forget Monte Carlo. We've got to stay calm and do enough in the return leg to get us into the final, and if there's a team that can do it, that team is us.'

Then, as they went off on their warm-up run, John Terry broke away from the group and came over.

'We made mistakes as well, Boss. We're just as much to blame,' he said.

'John,' I replied, 'we've got to look ahead. The important thing now is to get the right spirit back, because I believe we can do it and it's important that everyone in the dressing room believes it too. And you've got to help me. You're the vice-captain and your voice carries weight in there.'

At the end of the session there was a knock on

my door. It was Eidur Gudjohnsen. 'Boss, can I have a word? I'm sure we can do it, and we *will* do it!'

Maybe it was the very signal I was hoping to receive. The message had got through.

Newcastle v Chelsea, St James' Park, 25 April 2004

We were in with a great chance here, as Manchester United had lost their game the day before. There was still a mathematical possibility that we could win the title, though I knew perfectly well by now that Arsenal would be champions. But I was determined at all costs that we should come second, partly to avoid preliminary qualification for the Champions League competition next year, though more importantly to achieve a result that Chelsea had never managed since winning the title back in 1955. I always pick my teams to win, and we would try to win this time too, but even a draw would be more than welcome.

I knew beforehand that it would be very difficult, since we were going up there with no fewer than nine men missing, but when I saw how we kept on making mistakes, I was beside myself. A World Cup medal winner like Desailly, with all his experience, invites an opponent into a position where he can shoot with his one good foot. Amazing. It was a fine goal by Ameobi, but it could have been avoided. As for the goal by Shearer that put them ahead, no complaints. It was such a superb strike that I would have liked to run onto the pitch myself and shake his hand. And no complaints either at the reaction of my own players in the second half. Were it not for a miraculous reflex save by Shay Given to keep out Gudjohnsen's close-range header, a John Terry effort that hit the post in injury-time and a right-foot finish by Hasselbaink that just cleared the bar, the chances we created would have been enough to bring us level. The real problem was that we should never have found ourselves in such a situation. If we had ended the first-half 3–0 down, it would not have been unreasonable. Unfortunately we were too selfish in decisive situations, and paid the price.

What angered me more than the defeat on this occasion was the conduct of Robert Huth. Seeing him kick Alan Shearer while on the ground, I was furious. A young man still wet behind the ears at this level cannot and must not allow himself to do this kind of thing to a top-class player like Shearer. Back on the training ground I would have something to say to him, but even in the dressing room straight after the game I think he had already caught my drift. My English might be less than perfect, but I can manage to make myself pretty clear in these situations. I said as much to Peter Kenyon too. 'If I should still be here next year, a player like that I can do without.' I felt I had given him a lot of trust and plenty of chances, but I just did not like the way he had clearly got above himself. Becoming a player in the world of professional football means passing through a number of experiences, as in life itself, and inevitably making the odd mistake, but the blunder I saw him make at St James' Park was frankly unforgivable.

Fortunately my temper had subsided somewhat by the evening. Back in London, as soon as we landed, I changed hurriedly and dashed off to the Grosvenor House Hotel for the PFA Player of the Year awards. I was guest of honour, no less, and very proud to be invited. It was yet another demonstration of esteem and affection, helping to balance the opinions of those who seemed to have less and less faith in me. I even bought a new dinner jacket for the occasion, seeing that when I went to the wardrobe to dig out the one I had, my wife let me know her thoughts pretty plainly: 'Darling, I think it would be better if you went and bought yourself another one. You look like a waiter.'

Who knows how many opportunities there will be to wear it again? But I must say the new one did look much better on me. As soon as I arrived they led me to the top table and even asked me to say a few words. I took the opportunity to congratulate David Dein, whose Arsenal side had clinched the title that same afternoon, admitting that when at last we had managed to beat the Gunners in the Champions League I had hoped quietly for some sign of a psychological backlash that might have let us back into the Premiership race, but acknowledging that in their defeat of Liverpool they had shown character and personality that should be an example to every player present at the ceremony. As guest of honour I also had the pleasure of presenting Thierry Henry with the Players' Player award he so richly deserved. Frank Lampard had also been shortlisted for the award, but however much I might have wanted him to win, and however grateful

I might be for the extraordinary results his quality and consistency had produced this season, I would be the first to recognize that there was no doubt as to the rightful winner. Henry is phenomenal for his technique, his speed and his ability to score goals, but he is also a special young man. Polite, personable and very intelligent. And he shows it in many ways, not least in that he spent only six months playing in Italy and still speaks fluent Italian today. I know Mr Abramovich made attempts to lure him to Chelsea and it would have been a dream to have him, but I can understand that Arsenal would not even have thought about selling him. Neither was this the first time I had tried to sign him. When I was coach at Fiorentina, as an excuse to take the family out for the day, dine on fish somewhere and take a little sunshine at Monte Carlo, I went to the Louis II Stadium to take a close look at Lilian Thuram. At the end of the game, even my daughter had noticed how much the young Monaco striker Henry was overflowing with talent. The Fiorentina directors at the time, Giancarlo Antognoni and Oreste Cinquini, had already spoken to me about him. And they were absolutely right. I went to see the Monaco club president Vittorio Cecchi Gori on his yacht, hoping to convince him. I tried to whet his appetite: 'Listen, not only is Henry a fantastic player, but the way he moves, he reminds me of a young Cassius Clay.' No luck that time either, as he stayed with Monaco, but years later, in a recent interview he gave to an Italian newspaper, that remark of mine was made known to him and I know that he particularly liked the comparison.

252

It was a wonderful evening, during which my own Scott Parker was also named Young Player of the Year. I was very happy for him and not at all surprised, because this award simply confirmed the talent I saw in Scottie at the moment of wanting to sign him. There were other candidates from our team up for the award: John Terry, who would have been unlikely to win, since an established member of the national side will tend generally to be seen more as a veteran, and Glen Johnson, who perhaps was discounted by reason of the limited consistency he had been able to show. At all events, the significant number of Chelsea players in the reckoning will bear witness to the fact that we were building in the right direction. There was a delightful contribution from Harry Redknapp who took the microphone and held the floor with some very amusing stories, like the episode of Paulo Futré who arrived at West Ham insisting he would play only if he was given the number 10 shirt. I did not pick up all the niceties and nuances of the occasion, but enjoyed it greatly. I hope these traditions will never die out in England, and I was so happy at having been offered the chance to see them from the inside.

'You'll be here. I really do not think I will be. Maybe I'll drop in and see you, we'll have a coffee together'

Every book has a final chapter – an epilogue – and in this case, alas, it really is 'End of Story' . . . but only in a sporting sense of course, and against a background of farewells sweetened financially by the terms of our contracts. But there are also sentimental ties, which are particularly important to me. And so, aware that by the end of this month I would probably be drawing a line under my adventure with Chelsea, I knew it was going to be a very difficult time for me. Full of sadness, yes, but at least I would be secure in the knowledge that I had been guided by a clear conscience all the way.

If I were asked to sum up my feelings in a word, I would say I feel *proud*. Proud to be going with head held high, after taking on a challenge that was certainly not easy at the outset. Proud to have given a lot and received perhaps even more from a group of marvellous young men, my players during these four years, and from a veritable sea of supporters (a good metaphor for those waves of blue that fill the terraces). The reaction from most of them when I appeared for the first time at Stamford Bridge would have been 'Ranieri who?' And rightly so, because like Arsène Wenger I was a manager venturing into this fantastic world of football with a decent enough pedigree, but based on results too far removed from the Premier League to justify any immediate enthusiasm or optimism at my appointment. And then, to be adopted by them with so much warmth was the nicest possible recognition of my professional worth and the way I am as an individual. To leave all this behind would cost me dear, make no mistake. And to be leaving the club in the summer of 2004 would be still harder. If the parting of the ways had coincided with the change of ownership, I would have accepted it much more easily, but then again I would have missed out on a wonderfully intense year of activity. So much so that, however things might turn out in terms of results and contractual settlements, it would remain imprinted indelibly in the memory for the rest of my days.

Fortunately though, we had so many objectives of huge importance to pursue in this month of May that there was no time to stop and linger on thoughts such as these. Whatever happened – and I knew what would happen – all would be revealed at the end of a month that was destined to be unforgettable. It might be a dream come true, and it might not, but it was certainly not going to be ordinary.

Chelsea v Southampton, Stamford Bridge, 1 May 2004

In Italy, May Day is observed as the workers' holiday, one of those many days off from the office we have managed to invent for ourselves. We Italians certainly seem to have more than our fair share of public holidays in a year. But for now we were in England, my office was the dugout, and 1 May for us meant a home game with Southampton, a team which more recently, under Gordon Strachan, had given us problems more than once. But this time, whoever happened to be on the touchline (and I had the impression that Paul Sturrock was a more than worthy successor to his countryman), we absolutely had to beat them. I wanted to go to Old Trafford and face Manchester United with the advantage of being ahead of them in the table, but the Saints had a fine attack and I knew that it would be difficult. In Beattie, Pahars and Phillips they had players of power and speed, who could cause no small problems to my defence. Amongst other things, we had not had a win for five games – an unusual situation for us. This season, even when we had lost matches (not too often, thankfully) we had always managed to bounce back straight away. But it was no accident, in my view, that our barren spell had coincided with that magical night at Highbury. Not that I'm suggesting there were people who had got above themselves or dropped their guard – absolutely not – but in reality, even for a team like ours, assembled with high aims and expecting to win, it can happen that there is a psychological backlash from such an important result.

I hate having to mention it, but there was also a bit of bad luck involved. For example, it was true that we had not even managed a goal in our last two home games, although the fans would bear witness that we had created plenty of chances. Posts and crossbars had been hit, and miraculous saves pulled off by opposition goalkeepers. Neither had we any account to settle with the Blindfold Lady Justice, as our triumph over Arsenal was no gift. We had earned it fair and square.

In the dressing room before the match, I said to the team, 'Okay, apart from the Monaco game [which re-opens a personal wound for me], we haven't got too much to reproach ourselves with. You've continued to give it everything and created plenty of chances. But now the time has come to finish it off. This run-in period is too important for every one of us to risk undoing all that hard work and missing out on the satisfactions. It's all to play for this coming week. And since it all depends on us, let's start by winning today. I want absolutely no-one thinking about Wednesday. Our opponents today are Southampton, and this is the game we've got to win.'

All very true. Well ... almost. My mind was very much on the Monaco game, no question! To be honest, seeing the way we had gone down to defeat in the principality, I had not ceased thinking for an instant about how the mess might be put right. Obviously, with all this going on it had not even entered my head to speed up the return of Makelele and Gallas. Starting with Lampard in central midfield I had Geremi. Desailly was unavailable, so John Terry was partnered in central defence by Robert Huth. It was odd that I had been criticized for not drawing on the pool of youth players sufficiently and making the most of their talents. I would have thought the opposite was true, and Robert Huth was one of the best examples.

The first half was really not too pretty, and I went back into the dressing room saddened and a little worried. Not only had we been unable to end our home goal drought, but it was almost an exercise in nostalgia thinking about the last two games, when we had at least created some good chances albeit without managing to convert them. The scoreline, the play and the morale were not even anywhere near what I had hoped to see as we started our sprint for the line at the end of the season. Even so, I decided against making any half-time substitutions. No changes, just to give the lie to any predictable Tinkerman reactions. I wanted the team to react. I wanted them to find solutions. Followers of NBA basketball will know all about the coaching credentials of Phil Jackson. Winner of no less than nine champion rings during spells with the Chicago Bulls and the Los Angeles Lakers, he would never call time-out when seeing his team in difficulties, home or away. I am not a follower of his Zen philosophy, much less inspired by him, but like him I am convinced that a team – a football team in this case – has to find its own answers when faced with a problem. And this is what we had to do. Southampton were our play-off, our NBA final, given the importance of what awaited us after those remaining 45 minutes. John Terry and Frank Lampard like Michael Jordan and Scottie Pippen; Jesper

Gronkjaer and Wayne Bridge like Shaquille O'Neal and Kobe Bryant – bold comparisons technically speaking, but great champions all.

Well, there were no slam-dunks and no three-pointers in the second half, but my team put in a spectacular performance just the same. We needed a bit of luck to get ourselves started on this occasion, but after an own-goal by young Martin Crainie (who I felt a little sorry for, having discovered later that it was his Premiership debut), at last I saw what I was hoping to see: the ball in the net, certainly, but more especially the right attitude, conviction and fluency. A good performance from Joe Cole, an almost unstoppable Jesper Gronkjaer, and perfect chemistry between Gudjohnsen and Hasselbaink who were a continuous threat. And as he burst repeat-edly down the right, Gronkjaer was opening up gaps that Melchiot quickly took advantage of. Mario had not always played this year, because that is the way things are in the modern game with big squads. Glen Johnson is one of the biggest young European talents around, and I wanted to make the most of him straight away, but Melchiot had continued to be a firm choice for the first team. I wonder how many other squads in Europe can boast two right-backs of this quality? In effect, this pair perhaps best reflects our plan at the beginning of the season: to have two players of this quality and efficiency covering each position on the pitch. It was a shame that Mario had not gained the recognition from his Dutch national team this season that he deserved. He had been called up only for a friendly at the end of the season, but it wasn't enough for him to make the squad of 23 for Euro 2004. I know this boy is a real professional. I have seen his willingness, and his diligence in training, both before and after the compulsory sessions I organize with my staff. The work he does in the gym should be a lesson for everyone. Working out every day with weights will not make him a world-class footballer, certainly, but it says much about his mental approach. It so happens that our away fixture against the Saints earlier in the season was won with an invaluable goal by Mario, and that was not the only one of his Premiership campaign.

This time though, with a quarter of an hour left, the outcome was decided in the space of eight minutes by goals from Frank Lampard – who else? I had read and heard about people who were saying that Frank's recent performances had not been as decisive as a few weeks before. These were foolish and inexpert comments. Frank Lampard had always been decisive for us, and besides, could anyone be so blind as to miss the point that I had been asking him for a big physical effort, perhaps inordinately big, precisely because he was so fundamental to our cause and squad rotation had simply never applied in his case? My mind had told me several times to rest him. But then, instinct and the awareness of his value would soon persuade me otherwise. It was a sort of running internal debate on my part. A classic head-to-head situation.

In the end, it was Frank once again who had responded with actions, letting his feet do the talking on the pitch, to remind everyone that only a star like Thierry

Henry could have beaten him in the PFA vote for the title of Player of the Year.

A match, or at any rate, a second half like that could not have ended without serving up the classic cherry on the cake, in this instance the long-awaited return of Glen Johnson, who after coming on for Gudjohnsen promptly stepped up to score the fourth goal of the match.

I could hardly have left the stadium more contented, but now the problem was to take all the positives of those final 45 minutes against Southampton and transfer them to the clash with Monaco. Coming away from Stamford Bridge I let out a deep sigh. We had the weapons, and I would never lack the appetite for a tussle. Yes indeed, I felt ready for the challenge and I knew the team were with me all the way, in every sense.

The days leading up to a match as important as this can sometimes pose a little extra difficulty for teams to cope with, but not for a team with our experience and our objectives. Even press conferences are not ultimately a problem, despite the fact that there may be other issues – as indeed there were, in my particular case – not directly concerned with the game itself. The secret is knowing how to deal with them. I always try to be honest, never use clichés, and I am happy that most of the time my efforts are appreciated. And it was no different this time. There were the usual jokes with my friends the sharks, and although I made every effort to talk only about Monaco, it was inevitable that the odd question on my future would come up. Perfectly understandable, and all part of the game. The journalists would always shoot questions in the hope of grabbing a sensational headline for the morning edition, and I in turn would avoid saying anything remotely sensational.

'Claudio, do you think your future is going to be decided by the outcome of this match?' asked someone from the pack.

'Oh, come on my friend. I think we both know perfectly well what will happen here next year, regardless of how the game goes tomorrow . . .'

Diplomacy is all very well, but I was not going to sound like a visitor from another planet.

'You'll be here. I really do not think I will be. Maybe I'll drop in and see you, we'll have a coffee together.'

Cue general laughter as usual, and after doing the pre-match interview for UK television, as the match was being screened live, I dashed off to the airport to pick up my daughter Claudia who was taking advantage of a break from her university exams to come over to London with a friend to see the game. Another probable reason for the visit, I guessed, would be a shopping spree with her mother, but just to be able to see her was the best thing in the world, and for the moment Kenyon, Mourinho, Deschamps, Rothen and the rest were thrust very much down the order of priorities in my thoughts. No offence intended, naturally!

Claudia and her friend arrived almost on time, although they were greeted by an almighty downpour. On the way home, after chatting about her exams, Claudia asked me about the game, great football enthusiast that she is. In a certain sense, almost without realizing it, our roles were reversed and it was me telling her about my exams. At that moment my mobile rang. It was Jon Smith, my advisor at First Artist.

'Claudio, whatever did you say at that press conference today?'

I thought for a second, although there was really no need.

'Absolutely nothing! Why?'

He explained that he had received a call from Peter Kenyon, who had probably been told by someone or other that I wanted to leave Chelsea. The effect of wrongly reporting people's words had often led to the ruining of the best friendships (not the case here, obviously) and created the worst possible misunderstandings, but this seemed truly incredible. I was inclined to think many things of Peter Kenyon, but certainly not that he was stupid or disingenuous. How could he ever have thought (or wished) that I might decide to resign, giving up my contract and the hope – albeit slender – of staying in my job? Perhaps it was simply a ploy, a contractual move. Or maybe it really was a case of misreporting. In any event the matter was cleared up soon afterwards when Jon Smith called me again, saying that Kenyon had been in touch a second time and, having seen the report on Sky television, he realized there was nothing in it. Just a bit of confusion.

I was sorry not to be eating with Claudia and my wife that evening, but for a game of this importance I had decided on seclusion. I made my way to Chelsea Village, having booked Momo, a restaurant for them, up in town.

Food was about the last thing on my mind at that
moment. Not that Monaco had become an obsession,
but this really was more than just a football match. For
all of us. It represented the chance to realize our dreams
before time. The dreams of the team and of the fans.
My own dreams, and those of the club. So much had
been said about Roman Abramovich and his money, and
the ambitions that had understandably been growing
since the start of the season, but anyone who knows
anything about football would appreciate that to get to
where we were now had been a miracle. A miracle made
possible by our own professionalism, hard work and
passion. It was asking a lot, but now we had come this
far, theoretically ahead of our supposed timetable, we
could take this one step further. It would not be easy. In
fact, seeing the way things had gone in Monte Carlo it
would be almost impossible, but it was our duty to
try. Some of us would not be here next year – myself
and others, too – and so this game coming up the next
day was too big an opportunity for us not to be giving
any less than 200%. Should we succeed, it would be
an achievement to remember. Historic. If not, I had no
doubt my team would bow out with honour. Whatever
might happen, we had got ourselves into contention, and
this was a great thing in itself.

Leaving aside the declarations that had filtered
through the media, I suspected that Monaco, naturally
enough, would be looking to play a very canny game.
Covering tight at the back and in midfield, and ready to
attack on the break – they had the quality and speed to

do just that, especially with Rothen and Giuly. It had been reported that Jérôme Rothen was in poor shape due to a muscle strain, but my observer at their final training session assured me that he looked perfectly capable of making the game, and I knew he would be lining up against us. As far as my own team was concerned, there were two small doubts, but by the time we had finished our last training session at Harlington, before heading for the hotel, I had already made my decision. Faced with a choice between Melchiot and Johnson at right-back, I went for the Dutchman because, despite scoring against Southampton, Glen had played only a few minutes in that game. In midfield, on the other hand, I preferred to replace the suspended Makelele with Geremi rather than Parker, not least because of his greater experience in this particular kind of match. I knew perfectly well that central midfield was Scott's preferred position, also that I had not played him there too often and this would have been a good chance for him, but I was equally sure that by including Geremi I would give the team the right balance. Even for a well-equipped team like ours, it was a severe blow to lose Makelele, but this in turn highlights the positive side of having a big squad. As for the rest of the formation, I decided to go with the fittest, but also with the players I had most confidence in: Hasselbaink, Melchiot, Gudjohnsen, Terry, Lampard, Gronkjaer, Gallas. These were the players who over the years had never let me down, as individuals or as professionals. They were the ones who had brought us to where we were, and had earned the chance to play in a match that could make history. A match that perhaps had made history already.

Chelsea v Monaco, Champions League Semi-final, 2nd Leg, Stamford Bridge, 5 May 2004

Once again, at breakfast time on the morning of the match I could see that my players were prepared for the big occasion. They were pumped up to just the right level, but more importantly, focused and determined. This was going to be a very hard test for us, but just as with school exams, we had done all we could. We had studied thoroughly, and we were at ease.

From the window of my room, and through the picture window of the restaurant when we came down for our tea and toast, I could see crowds of fans gathering around the stadium. Fantastic, this enthusiasm. At that moment it was just as I always liked to say on my page of the programme notes sold at the ground on match days. Together with all our hearts. It is a wonderful sensation, especially because it is so positive. It generates an incredible electricity. When we ran onto the field for the warm-up, the fans were all there waiting on the terraces, already shouting for us. Marvellous. As the players went through their exercises with Roberto Sassi, either with the ball or jumping obstacles, before doing a few more sprints, I almost allowed myself to daydream for an instant. Casting my eyes around the four sides of the stadium, at that moment I was practically able to absorb all of that force, that flow of energy coming from the terraces. I had to try and win this for them too. We all had to. Then a few seconds later I saw that the warm-up was nearly finished and I looked around to catch Gary Staker's eye and give him a nod. Gary is the player liaison officer, but so much more for every one of the team, and certainly he had been for me. He is an extraordinary man whose dedication to Chelsea FC is total. His mother was Italian, and on the language side he had been invaluable to me, just as he had been in the past for all the other Italians, from Gianluca Vialli onwards, who had arrived at Stamford Bridge with only a limited command of English. But to think of Gary only as a translator or interpreter would be both inaccurate and ungenerous. During all these years in London he had been my guardian angel. One of those people who remain unseen, but have a decisive bearing on the success of the team. I hope that Chelsea will never lose an individual as important as this.

I had not asked anything particularly complicated of him that evening, but I wanted him to give me a hand with something. I had made some colour photocopies of the Champions League trophy, and before the team came back in from the warm-up, Gary's part in the plan was to pin up a copy on the locker of each player. When they came back in to put on their match strip before being called into the tunnel by the referee, they were surprised to see these pictures of the cup that had appeared suddenly in their individual places. This was the reaction I wanted. Some of them were still looking at the image when I said, 'This is the dream we all have when we start out, longing to be professional footballers. Now you're really near, in a position where thousands of players have never been, and there's no guarantee that you'll ever get there again in your careers. Let's not waste this chance. Let's try and get hold of this cup. Come on! Let's go and find a way into this all-holy final! Go for it!'

Photocopies or no photocopies, the team played from the very first minute with unbelievable intensity, determination and courage. With a good part of the crowd barely settled in their seats, we had already had our first chance through Hasselbaink. Their goalkeeper, Flavio Roma, responded well, and it would turn out to be just the first superb save of a brilliant night for him. In the first half alone he pulled off two absolute miracles, one from Jimmy's effort and another from a powerful long-range drive by Lampard. In the end, they were two saves that made the difference. In answer to a question at the pre-match press conference, I had said we would need two things in equal measure: the aggression and breakneck pace that typified English sides of the 1970s and 80s, and the rational approach of an Italian side. And this is exactly what we did, as we had them on the ropes up to the hour mark while giving them practically nothing. Only on one occasion did I have a real scare. As Morientes cut through the middle and ran towards Carlo, I shut my eyes. Happily he put the chance just wide, but as we found out later in the second half, you just do not give opportunities like that to a player of his calibre. In the 22rd minute we took the lead in the most spectacular way imaginable. Gronkjaer had the ball on the right, but instead of making for the by-line and crossing right-footed, he opted to turn and cut in toward the middle before releasing a magnificent left-foot cross that looped over goalkeeper Roma and lodged into the top corner at the far post. At that moment a thought flashed through my mind: his goal against Liverpool in our final match of the 2002/03 Premiership season that ushered in the modern era of Chelsea Football Club . . . the Champions League, the arrival of Abramovich, the great buying campaign and the new stature of the Blues. It was not the same end of the pitch where Jesper had scored last year, but the similarities were too strong for the two events not to come together in my mind. Perhaps unconsciously I was hoping for the same happy ending. In reality of course he had meant to cross the ball, and it was certainly not a shot on goal (against Liverpool, it had been a genuine goal attempt), but need we tell anybody?

Having scored, we continued to push forward, keeping the tempo high, because the deficit over the two legs had been halved and, though there was still some way to go, we were just one goal away from the final. But neither could we afford to concede, and my worry now was that the boys might get carried away with enthusiasm and leave themselves exposed at the back. In fact I was more worried by this than by the need to score another. Our attacking game was so fluent and we were creating so many chances that we simply had to get the ball in the net. At the same time, whilst the threat of Giuly and his speed of execution had been one of my more serious concerns, he was making relatively limited impact in

270

attack, and although Rothen was having a great game on
the left, belying his supposed lack of fitness as reported
during the build-up, we had allowed them nothing apart
from the shot by Morientes.

Looking at my watch, I saw that half-time was only a
couple of minutes away. Just as I was thinking it would
be a good situation to go in at the interval a goal up,
have a bit of a rest and a talk, then come out in the
second half and look for the one that would take us
through, the dream scenario materialized. A link-up
between Melchiot, Gudjohnsen and Bridge was finished
off by Lampard with surgical precision. It was the best
practical application of what they had been through time
and time again at Harlington. 'Pass and move!' Who
knows how many times I had shouted it at them, and this
time they had performed it to perfection. Whether it was
my personal enthusiasm or whether Stamford Bridge
really was shaking with the shouts of joy from the fans, I
could not say, but it was an incredible sensation. Anger
and elation at one and the same time. Human and sporting reactions. As it stood then, we were through. We
were in the final! The ghosts of the away leg had been
blown away. But it was an illusion, and all too brief. In
the two minutes that followed, I swear it never entered
my head that a berth in the final had already been
secured. I am not stupid, and I know my football too
well. There was not even time to conjure up such a pipe
dream. We were hit by the worst thing that can happen
to any team, both in the practical sense, and mentally.
A goal deep into injury-time. I cannot say that if we

had gone in 2–0 up at half-time, it would have been us going to Gelsenkirchen, but for Monaco to score at that particular moment, and in the way they did, was a killer. Rothen did brilliantly well to peel away and accelerate down the left, and Ibarra was lightning quick in the six-yard box. In all probability he knocked the ball over the line with his arm rather than with his chest, but if the referee and his assistants saw nothing irregular, these are regrets that count for relatively little. The players protested, but apart from Gronkjaer, who received a yellow card for his pains, their complaints were no more than half-hearted. The shock and disappointment were too much, and that was the worst part. In reality the game was still wide open. With another goal we could have taken it into extra-time, and we were still playing great football with all our fans behind us. I said as much to the team during the interval, although I would have been the first to acknowledge the enormity of the task. Players are not machines, and to be on the point of going in at half-time with the tie almost won, then knocked out a few seconds later by a goal that probably should have been disallowed, was a terrible blow.

At the beginning of the second half we had a huge chance to score a third. Seeing how the team had played the first 45 minutes, I obviously made no changes, whereas Deschamps took off Squillaci and replaced him with Plasil in midfield, putting Ibarra back into his customary right-back position. They had still probably not found the right combination when Wayne Bridge managed to break through down the left flank and send a ball across the middle that neither Gudjohnsen first nor Gronkjaer after him were able to knock in. It was a great chance, and was probably the coup de grâce for us. With fifteen minutes of the half gone, Rothen on the left and Morientes in the middle produced what I have to admit was a splendid combination ending in a great goal, and it was game over, with Monaco through to the final. Deservedly so too, though looking back on the two legs of the tie, we had many regrets.

It was 2–2 and by now the players were tired, as well as demoralized. I made three changes, bringing on Johnson, Crespo and Parker, but it made no difference. Our European fairy-tale was over, there and then. I had always said that the Champions League was a sort of bonus for us, and that our main objective was the Premiership title. True enough, but we had come this far, and to have to get off at the last stop before the Grand Terminus, with so many different thoughts as to what might have been, well, frankly it left a very bitter taste. Having done the usual interviews, I left the ground with my family and my close friends who naturally had come to London to see the game. I am not one to get over-excited about victories, and neither do I get too upset over defeats. To have my wife Rosanna, my daughter Claudia and my friends around me was all I wanted at that particular moment. We went to eat at Scalini's, as we often did after a match, and it was a wonderful evening. As we walked in, everyone applauded straight away. This is something that would never happen in Italy after being knocked out of a competition. I am not

sure what I felt. Touched? Perhaps even embarrassed?
No matter. The Redknapps were there too, father and
son, and they came up to greet me and congratulate me.
This made me especially happy as I have an enormously
high regard for them both. Harry is a fine manager who
has always succeeded in achieving more than the quality
of the teams available to him might promise, and Jamie
has been dogged by misfortune. Had he been spared all
those injuries in the course of his career, he would have
been one of the best footballers in the world for at least a
decade. He has a vision and a technical ability possessed
only by the best footballers in the game. A player like
this, you simply have to admire.

Picking ourselves up after the let-down of Europe was
not easy, but perhaps we were fortunate in that just two
days later we had another vitally important fixture. The
last big challenge. Manchester United at Old Trafford.
It was better we should face them straight away, as a
game against less exalted opposition at this juncture,
however important the result, might just have tempted
us to ease off a little. Playing Manchester United away,
this obviously was not an option. I had said it over and
over again: second place was a must. Now was the time
to front up and play for it.

Before leaving for Manchester, something occurred
which was really rather surprising, in view of the situation. I had a meeting with Roman Abramovich at the
office lasting over an hour. He wanted to hear my
thoughts on how the team could be improved for next
season. Now, I am grown up, vaccinated against tropical

diseases, and frankly there is little that can surprise me any more, but this conversation could have given me more than one reason to think I might be able to stay in my job next year. So, I addressed the topic openly and with every respect for the chairman, with whom, I repeat, I had always had a very satisfactory professional and personal relationship.

'Roman, why do you want to get rid of me now? I could have understood it last July when you arrived, but after the season we've just had I find it a bit harder to see why.'

Perhaps he had not been expecting my question, or maybe he simply did not have a ready answer. He looked at me a moment, then smiled.

'Look Claudio, as of now, nothing has been decided. There's been no contract with any other coach even discussed, let alone signed. I want to think about it carefully, look at the options and then make a choice on how and with whom to plan the future of Chelsea, when I'm ready.'

It was his prerogative, naturally, but even if the conversation seemed to leave a door open for me, it was a door apparently letting in no more than a very narrow chink of light.

Manchester United v Chelsea, Old Trafford, 8 May 2004

Before arriving at the stadium, I reminded the players how Arsenal had shown themselves to be a team of champions in the manner they had responded to being knocked out of the Champions League by us. Now I was expecting that we would be capable of doing the same thing. 'It's a year in which we've been struggling to do something memorable in the history of Chelsea. The Champions League is a gamble, but the domestic League is the history, the character and the life of a team.'

For the first time since the Stuttgart game I had selected a 4–5–1 line-up with Gudjohnsen the lone striker and Lampard and Gronkjaer just behind him. And it was Jesper who gave us the lead following a corner-kick, this time shooting from the opposite side of the pitch to when he scored the goal against Monaco. It was another spectacular goal, and an extremely telling one in the situation, which I hoped would persuade him to try his luck a little more often in future. Not an easy season this, for Jesper, given the illness of his mother, but he had been exceptional in the way he handled his personal worries and his pain, and continued to honour his professional commitments. A wonderful footballer, but a very sensitive young man too, who might also be leaving Chelsea at the end of the season, and if this were to happen – obviously with yours truly no longer around – I hope he will find the good fortune he deserves.

The match was played in far from summery weather conditions. Rain, wind and typically northern temperatures, but I was not bothered. It was almost the ideal setting for a contest of this nature. At the beginning of the year, after reading our calendar of fixtures, I had confided to a friend, 'If we're going to win the Premiership title, we'll do it on the penultimate day at Old Trafford!' I had made my debut as Chelsea manager at the famous stadium with a nice 3–3 draw, and we had done very well ever since up there, achieving some great results. Now I wanted to round off my adventure with a result that would at least be the one I had so hoped for, given that the title was out of reach. Even after taking the lead it was a hard, hard game. United changed their formation several times, bringing on Louis Saha and switching to 4–3–3 with an inspired Cristiano Ronaldo popping up on both wings. In the first half, the referee also awarded the home side a perfectly valid penalty that could have changed the complexion of the game completely, but St Cudicini came to the rescue. Carlo dipped into his repertoire and pulled out one of the best saves of his Chelsea career, denying Van Nistelrooy from the spot. In the second half though, the Dutchman continued to be a thorn in our side and his contribution was decisive in putting Manchester back in contention. First he drew Robert Huth into committing a foul that brought the German a second yellow card, and we were left with ten men for the last 17 minutes; then he profited from a moment of indecision between Cudicini and Terry to score the equalizer.

At that point it became hard. Away to Manchester United with ten men. And if they had secured the three points, they could still have had an outside chance of beating us to second place. I had already brought on Glen Johnson in place of Melchiot, putting him in the middle with Gronkjaer wide on the right in defence. Then I made another change after the goal, putting on

Scott Parker for Joe Cole, with Geremi going to right-back and Gronkjaer returning to midfield. Sir Alex Ferguson in his turn threw Kleberson and Solskjaer into the fray, but even with a man less, it was the determination of my team that had made the difference, playing in their Theatre of Dreams. When referee Steve Bennett blew the final whistle, it was a huge satisfaction. A purely private moment. Just a few seconds when I cut myself off from everything. I had done it. We had done it. That second place was now a reality and it was so very important to me. I say it again. I know there are no trophies or medals for second place, but for us it was essential. In any case, at the beginning of the season Roman Abramovich really had not asked me to win any medals, even if it was implicit that we would have tried our hardest on all fronts. And yet, no obligation. But this second place was important. Significant. It proved that we had been bettered only by an extraordinary Arsenal side. It also meant exemption from preliminary qualifying for next year's Champions League competition, but the most important thing for me was that in the midst of many and various difficulties we had reached a position never achieved by Chelsea since the mid 1950s. All these things meant so much to me. And in a certain sense the best was yet to come, as after shaking hands with Sir Alex and a few of his players, and embracing a few of my own, the sporting tradition of English football managed to surprise me yet again. As I walked along the touchline toward the tunnel that led back to the dressing rooms, I saw that almost all the Manchester United fans had stayed in their places to wait for me. To applaud me and to congratulate me. How marvellous! They were showing their appreciation just as all the football supporters in England had accepted me and valued my efforts. Over the last few months I had received hundreds of letters from all sorts of places and from all the fan clubs in the land, expressing their affection and their solidarity for the situation I had been living with. I might lose Chelsea, but never, I think, the respect of these people. Yet another pearl in the collection of my experiences in this country, which has managed to surprise me pleasantly at pretty well every turn. Wherever my professional career may take me, I will never tire of encouraging anyone involved in coaching or playing the game to experience feelings like these. In the world of sport, I think there can be no contradiction more obvious than the inconsistency between the image of English football and English fans, and the actual reality. People who go on about hooligans do not know what they are saying. Having been coach at Chelsea for four wonderful years, I can find nothing but good to say. Not just about our own fans – that would be too easy – but about all fans in this country, the loyalty and the passion they have for the game here, and the way it is lived out so spontaneously.

As I fastened my seat belt on the plane that brought us back to London, I could not have been happier. We really had achieved something. I felt the warmth of people from all sides, and even if my future at the helm of Chelsea was more or less decided, bar the official announcement, I was genuinely at peace.

Chelsea v Leeds, Stamford Bridge, 15 May 2004

We were mathematically safe in second place in the table. Leeds, likewise, were by now mathematically relegated to the First Division. So it was a friendly in everything but name, although this would never be the right word to describe a fixture between Chelsea and Leeds. Call it a passing-out parade, at least for us, seeing as we had earned it. All the same, there could never have been a game so pointless in terms of the result, and yet so important to me personally. It would be my last game in charge of Chelsea. How would I react? How could I not be affected? How would I take leave of the fans? What kind of a send-off would they and the team give me? All these questions were whirring around in my head, and really and truly, I had no answer to them. For the first time ever, I did not even go out onto the pitch for the warm-up. I stayed in my dressing room, concentrating quietly, living out these last two hours as manager of Chelsea. A break with habit providing confirmation, no doubt, that the game about to start was not going to be like other games, and would have a particular emotional impact on me. Such was the tension that I had to control it – or at least I attempted to – by chewing vigorously on gum throughout the match. Not the most attractive of habits, and something I hardly ever do.

In reality it was not a great game, although I thought the team looked good, but for the record we won with a goal by Jesper Gronkjaer, who was absolutely red hot in these final few games of the season. True enough, the result counted for little, although not in everyone's view. I for one wanted to go out as a winner. The show really began – and not only for me – about four minutes into the second half. The entire stadium began chanting my name, and never stopped right through until the end. It was something I would never have expected. The chants went on and on, becoming louder and louder. I literally did not know what to do, but I was deeply touched. I would have liked to thank them all in some way at the end of the game, but I really did not know how.

During the second half I brought on Alexis Nicolas, and more importantly I gave a spell to Mario Stanic, who really deserved it. Mario had suffered endless problems with his knee this year, but never for a moment did he give up, and his professional conduct had been an example to the whole team, in the truest sense. Every morning he would turn up to train with us at Harlington, and when prevented by his troublesome leg from carrying on, he would go and work out in the gym. Every afternoon without fail, he went along to Chelsea Village for physiotherapy. Always and everywhere he had helped the players to bond in the dressing room, and in everything we achieved this season, he had played a part. At the beginning of the season he could have gone to West Ham, where obviously he would have had many more opportunities to play, but he told me he would rather stay, and I was more than happy to keep him. He has played for Chelsea in just about every position on the pitch, and never complained, even when I asked him to play at full-back. The fact is that he is a hugely talented footballer with a fine physique, and with these qualities he has always been able to play anywhere. Spain, Belgium, Italy, England . . . Stanic has always scored plenty of goals, and important goals too. It is a shame his injury prevented me from playing him more often, because even in a squad with the strength and depth of ours, he would always be a very useful addition.

At the end of the game there was applause for everyone, and a well-deserved ovation for John Terry and Frank Lampard. They have been truly phenomenal this year, but best of all they represent the real future of this team. A bright future too, as there is nothing missing. The club has both money and the will to achieve. A great group of players have come through, many of them young, and with the right attitude to ensure progress. There is a splendid army of fans, who have never created problems or generated controversy, but simply helped their team. And then there is the magnificent, historic ground with facilities that are improving all the time. The problem was simply that I would no longer be a part of it all, and this was heart-breaking, although as far as the history of the club is concerned it could be totally unimportant, even though I like to think that I might have been the one to pull all these threads together and weave them into a tapestry of top honours. Goodbyes are always sad and can sometimes be a touch schmaltzy. But the adieu at the end of the Leeds game was wonderful. I had not planned anything by way of a thank you to the fans, as I wanted it to be spontaneous, just as the relationship between us had always been. I had thought maybe of going out into the middle and saluting the four corners of the terraces, but I would have been too far away. A few words? Spy would certainly have passed me the microphone had I asked him, but my English would not have allowed me to express what I really felt at that particular moment. So in the end, I did a walk around the pitch, trying to stay as near to them all as possible. Somebody threw me a scarf, which I put around my neck straight away. This club and its colours really felt as if they belonged, and I was honoured, even though it was the last time I would wear blue and white in this stadium. My stadium. I managed to keep a stiff upper lip – well, pretty much – and this was an achievement in itself. In fact I was deliberately trying to stay cool, as I wanted to miss nothing of all this. I wanted to take it all in. Then I realized that perhaps the team had prepared a farewell for me, as Gary, close by, was trying to delay me and keep me out there until something or other was ready. And in fact, as I completed my circuit, the players came out onto the pitch again and formed two lines for me to walk through. A real guard of honour. Marvellous, and surely unique. The wonderful thing about it all was the spontaneity. The spontaneity of relationships built on true feelings. Relationships with everyone. Team, staff, fans, journalists and the owner too.

After the handshakes, the interviews and the goodbyes in the dressing room and in the tunnel, my wife joined me and we went off to the buffet Roman Abramovich had laid on at the Health Club to celebrate the end of the season. We were crossing the field when at a certain point Rosanna said 'Claudio, take one last look at your stadium!' I stopped a moment, and it was a moment to savour. A wonderful picture postcard I would always remember. Beautiful sunshine, empty terraces. An almost unreal silence, and I drank it in. Strange to relate, as we made small talk over a cocktail, Roman asked me 'So when do the players come back now?' I looked at him, smiled and answered straight off: 'That depends when the new coach wants them.' He was lost for words for a second, then we both laughed. Out into the car park before driving home, I signed what seemed like a thousand autographs. They were all waiting there and I was not going to disappoint anyone.

A fortnight later, it was official: 'Claudio Ranieri is to leave the club. Claudio has done a first-class job for the club and has paved the way for future success. We would like to wish Claudio all the best for the future.'

In the end, after all the months of speculation carried by the media and the press far and wide, this was the statement given to the public. I was in Italy, Peter Kenyon was in Portugal and directors Eugene Tenenbaum and Bruce Buck were in London. Peter called Jon Smith, my advisor in London, to arrange a meeting/conference call with me, Buck, Tenenbaum and Smith, when Tenenbaum and Smith were to tell me their decision. Of course Jon Smith asked the purpose of the call and Kenyon told him. Jon then called up agent Vicenzo Morabito, who happens to be a friend of mine, asking him to give me the news. When Vicenzo made his call to me ('It looks as if I'm the one who's got to give you the bad news . . .') it obviously came as no surprise. This was then followed up with a conference call to Smith, his brother Phil, Tenenbaum and Buck, all of whom were at the Chelsea office in Stamford Bridge, while I was in Rome. It would have been better if we could have had a meeting at Stamford Bridge. I would have been able to hold a final press conference as manager, just as Gerard Houllier had been able to do at Anfield before he left. But they had already agreed terms with Jose Mourinho and wanted to tell me the news before the appointment of the new manager leaked to the press.

A final verdict? From a personal point of view, entirely positive, as I have said before. These four years of my life have absolutely flown past, which must mean it has been a happy time. Obviously I would like to have won much more. In fact I would like to have won something. Period. Something to put in the showcase – at least a trophy more prestigious than the cup we won pre-season in Malaysia. Instead, I can list a historic second place in the League, a Champions League semi-final and an FA Cup final, which is not a bad return when seen against the technical and financial background of my four-year tenure. I leave only with the regret of the cup tie against Monaco. Today, as I sit on the terrace of my Parioli home here in Rome, writing the last few lines of this account, I feel certain we would not have lost the Monte Carlo leg had I been unaware of that meeting between the club and Mourinho's agent the evening before. I wanted to win at any cost, and allowed my emotions to rule my actions. It is my only regret. I realize that

I gave in to a weakness, and therefore it was my own fault. But I also regret not having had Emmanuel Petit available this season; with all due respect to everyone else, his absence was one of the reasons we did not win. I know that his class and his leadership would have been decisive.

The first two years were spent making changes to the team, rejuvenating a squad that had been put together by Gullit and taken on to success by Vialli. It was not easy to start a new cycle and take on the responsibility of having to shed historic players like Wise, Poyet, Leboeuf, De Goey and Ferrer. Even before the Abramovich millions materialized we had been improving steadily, year on year, to the point of qualifying for the Champions League in 2003. This proves that we had always been on the right track, and were setting very solid foundations. I feel sure I will leave a legacy in the dressing room, an ethic of sacrifice in training and the will to keep improving. I am leaving behind a fine group of players, and a philosophy of life, I think, if this does not sound too presumptuous.

At the same time I am taking away so many good things. Memories first and foremost. Human relationships, and the experience gained from being four years in this other world. The way the English fans see their football. Respect for others, and for the high ideal in sport. The will to bounce back after defeats and get back quickly to winning ways. Never going over the top, whether in disappointment or in victory.

A week after the end of the Premiership campaign, as

it happens, I met Roman Abramovich again in Milan, and I must say I had to ask myself why. Had he really not decided yet? Did it depend on the outcome of the Champions League final? No doubt it did. But as far as I was concerned it was a situation that all seemed rather pointless, as indeed it turned out. Even a little senseless.

And how do I judge my relationship with Roman Abramovich, in the end? Marvellous! He is everything a coach would want his chairman to be. Never interfering with selections, not expecting to win every single game, willing to buy more players than you ask for, and always wearing a smile. Of course he wants a plan for success, and wants to see the team play attractive football, but this is absolutely normal. As first-time chairman of a football club, I would say he has passed the test with full marks. I believe he trusted me a lot. I consider him an intelligent man, otherwise he could never have achieved all that he has in just 37 years. I see someone with the ability to understand whoever he finds in front of him. On the human level, I find it a little more difficult to portray him, since he speaks only Russian and a few words of English. I should say he communicates more than anything with his smile. He impresses with deeds, and here I am not talking about money. I am thinking about the time he gave me a lift to Rome in his aircraft, another time when he offered to do the same again, and the time he invited us all onto his yacht after the disappointment of Monte Carlo. These were real acts of generosity, not merely image-building stunts. The group is important to him. He thinks the team should be managed by someone with a winning record, and in the end I think this is the main reason why he took the decision to change his coach. But our relationship was always sincere, and personally I will always have a good memory of it. And of his entourage too. Of Peter Kenyon, not so good; we were never on the same wavelength, probably because I do not know very much about marketing, and he does not know a great deal about matters on the field of play.

In any event, Chelsea is certainly destined to grow. I am confident of having sown good seed, and now it will be important to water it well and take good care of the harvest. Of course I would have liked to reap the fruits myself, but one way or another, as a friend and a fan of the club, I will be able to do so from a distance. I would never presume to think I know how to win better than anyone else, since it has already happened in my career that I have done the building work and then others have then come along after me and done a great job, as Hector Cuper did at Valencia. Even so, I say it again, I would have liked to stay and had the chance to win for myself.

As for the players, I embrace them all in my imagination, as there is honestly not one that did not give everything he had for me, and consequently for the club. Only Christian Panucci clashed with this group of players in terms of attitude, and in fact he was not with me for long.

Proud at having brought on Lampard and Terry? Well, there is always pride, but a coach is a father figure who speaks to everyone in the same way and looks to develop the qualities of every individual for the common

good. The rest is up to the individuals themselves. John
Terry and Frank Lampard were already top players
before working with me, as they had the right qualities
within them. Perhaps I saw those qualities before they
did and helped to bring them out. I will always follow
their progress and have a soft spot for them, as they have
become a part of me.

'Now I am grown up, vaccinated against tropical diseases, and frankly there is little that can surprise me any more'

CLAUDIO RANIERI FACTFILE

Date of Birth: 20 October 1951
Birthplace: Rome, Italy
Wife: Rosanna
Children: Daughter Claudia

Signed for AS Roma in 1969, later moving to Catanzaro and Catania, making a total of over 350 appearances in Serie A and B. Went on to coach Vigor Lamenzia and manage lower-division club Campania before moving to Cagliari.

MANAGERIAL RECORD

Cagliari

1988/89	Serie C 1st Place	P34 W16 D13 L5	Promoted from Serie C to Serie B
1989/90	Serie B 3rd Place	P38 W17 D 13 L8	Promoted from Serie B to Serie A
1990/91	Serie A 14th Place	P34 W6 D17 L11	

Napoli
Joined 1991

1991/92	Serie A 4th Place	P34 W15 D12 L7
1992/93	Serie A 11th Place	P34 W10 D12 L12

Fiorentina
Joined 1993

1993/94	Serie B 1st Place	P38 W17 D16 L5	Promoted to Serie A
1994/95	Serie A 10th Place	P34 W12 D11 L11	

CLAUDIO RANIERI

1995/96	Serie A 4th Place	P34 W17 D8 L9	Coppa Italia and Supercoppa Italia winner
1996-97	Serie A 9th Place	P34 W10 D15 L9	

Valencia
Joined 19 September 1997 after Valencia had lost their first three games.

1997/98	Primera Liga 9th Place	P35 W16 D7 L12	
1998/99	Primera Liga 4th Place	P38 W19 D8 L11	Spanish Cup winner

Atlético Madrid
Joined 27 June 1999

1999/2000   Primera Liga 17th Place*
*On leaving 3 September 2000

Chelsea
Joined 18 September 2000

2000/01	Premiership 6th Place	P32 W16 D7 L9	
2001/02	Premiership 6th Place	P38 W17 D13 L8	FA Cup Runners-Up
2002/03	Premiership 4th Place	P38 W19 D10 L9	
2003/04	Premiership 2nd Place	P38 W24 D7 L7	

Overall Chelsea Premiership record under Ranieri: P146 W76 (52%) D37(25%) L33(23%)

CHELSEA RESULTS 2003/04

13/08/2003	Champions League	3rd QR 1st Leg	SK Zilina	0 2	Chelsea
17/08/2003	Premiership		Liverpool	1 2	Chelsea
23/08/2003	Premiership		Chelsea	2 1	Leicester City
26/08/2003	Champions League	3rd QR 2nd Leg	Chelsea	3 0	SK Zilina
30/08/2003	Premiership		Chelsea	2 2	Blackburn Rovers
13/09/2003	Premiership		Chelsea	4 2	Tottenham Hotspur
16/09/2003	Champions League	Group G	Sparta Prague	0 1	Chelsea
20/09/2003	Premiership		Wolverhampton Wanderers	0 5	Chelsea
27/09/2003	Premiership		Chelsea	1 0	Aston Villa
01/10/2003	Champions League	Group G	Chelsea	0 2	Besiktas
05/10/2003	Premiership		Middlesbrough	1 2	Chelsea
14/10/2003	Premiership		Birmingham City	0 0	Chelsea
18/10/2003	Premiership		Arsenal	2 1	Chelsea
22/10/2003	Champions League	Group G	Chelsea	2 1	Lazio
25/10/2003	Premiership		Chelsea	1 0	Manchester City

FACTFILE

Date	Competition	Round	Home			Away
29/10/2003	Carling Cup	3rd Round	Chelsea	4	2	Notts County
01/11/2003	Premiership		Everton	0	1	Chelsea
04/11/2003	Champions League	Group G	Lazio	0	4	Chelsea
09/11/2003	Premiership		Chelsea	5	0	Newcastle United
22/11/2003	Premiership		Southampton	0	1	Chelsea
26/11/2003	Champions League	Group G	Chelsea	0	0	Sparta Prague
30/11/2003	Premiership		Chelsea	1	0	Manchester United
03/12/2003	Carling Cup	4th Round	Reading	0	1	Chelsea
06/12/2003	Premiership		Leeds United	1	1	Chelsea
09/12/2003	Champions League	Group G	Besiktas	0	2	Chelsea
13/12/2003	Premiership		Chelsea	1	2	Bolton Wanderers
17/12/2003	Carling Cup	5th Round	Aston Villa	2	1	Chelsea
20/12/2003	Premiership		Fulham	0	1	Chelsea
26/12/2003	Premiership		Charlton Athletic	4	2	Chelsea
28/12/2003	Premiership		Chelsea	3	0	Portsmouth
03/01/2004	FA Cup	3rd Round	Watford	2	2	Chelsea
07/01/2004	Premiership		Chelsea	0	1	Liverpool
11/01/2004	Premiership		Leicester City	0	4	Chelsea
14/01/2004	FA Cup	3rd Round Replay	Chelsea	4	0	Watford
18/01/2004	Premiership		Chelsea	0	0	Birmingham City
24/01/2004	FA Cup	4th Round	Scarborough	0	1	Chelsea
01/02/2004	Premiership		Blackburn Rovers	2	3	Chelsea
08/02/2004	Premiership		Chelsea	1	0	Charlton Athletic
11/02/2004	Premiership		Portsmouth	0	2	Chelsea
15/02/2004	FA Cup	5th Round	Arsenal	2	1	Chelsea
21/02/2004	Premiership		Chelsea	1	2	Arsenal
25/02/2004	Champions League	1st Round 1st Leg	VfB Stuttgart	0	1	Chelsea
28/02/2004	Premiership		Manchester City	0	1	Chelsea
09/03/2004	Champions League	1st Round 2nd Leg	Chelsea	0	0	VfB Stuttgart
13/03/2004	Premiership		Bolton Wanderers	0	2	Chelsea
20/03/2004	Premiership		Chelsea	2	1	Fulham
24/03/2004	Champions League	Quarter Final 1st Leg	Chelsea	1	1	Arsenal
27/03/2004	Premiership		Chelsea	5	2	Wolverhampton Wanderers
03/04/2004	Premiership		Tottenham Hotspur	0	1	Chelsea
06/04/2004	Champions League	Quarter Final 2nd Leg	Arsenal	1	2	Chelsea
10/04/2004	Premiership		Chelsea	0	0	Middlesbrough

12/04/2004 Premiership	Aston Villa	3	2	Chelsea
17/04/2004 Premiership	Chelsea	0	0	Everton
20/04/2004 Champions League Semi-Final 1st Leg	AS Monaco	3	1	Chelsea
25/04/2004 Premiership	Newcastle United	2	1	Chelsea
01/05/2004 Premiership	Chelsea	4	0	Southampton
05/05/2004 Champions League Semi-Final 2nd Leg	Chelsea	2	2	AS Monaco
08/05/2004 Premiership	Manchester United	1	1	Chelsea
15/05/2004 Premiership	Chelsea	1	0	Leeds United

Player Appearances and Goals

Premiership

Player	Apps	Subs	Goals
Frank Lampard	38	0	10
John Terry	33	0	2
Wayne Bridge	33	0	1
Claude Makelele	26	4	
Carlo Cudicini	26	0	
William Gallas	23	6	
Jimmy Floyd Hasselbaink	22	8	13
Adrian Mutu	21	4	6
Mario Melchiot	20	3	2
Jesper Gronkjaer	19	12	2
Sorele Fotso Ndjitap Geremi	19	6	1
Joe Cole	18	17	1
Eidur Gudjohnsen	17	9	6
Damien Duff	17	6	5
Glen Johnson	17	2	3
Marcel Desailly	15	0	
Hernan Crespo	13	6	10
Robert Huth	8	8	
Marco Ambrosio	8	0	
Scott Parker	7	4	1
Celestine Babayaro	5	1	1
Juan Sebastian Veron	5	2	1
Neil Sullivan	4	0	
Emmanuel Petit	3	1	
Alexis Nicolas	1	1	
Mario Stanic	0	2	
Filipe de Oliveira	0	1	

FACTFILE

FA Cup

Player	Apps	Subs	Goals
Frank Lampard	4	0	1
William Gallas	4	0	
Jesper Gronkjaer	4	0	
Adrian Mutu	3	0	3
Jimmy Floyd Hasselbaink	3	0	1
John Terry	3	0	1
Mario Melchiot	3	0	
Carlo Cudicini	3	0	
Claude Makelele	3	0	
Eidur Gudjohnsen	2	2	2
Joe Cole	2	1	
Celestine Babayaro	2	0	
Wayne Bridge	2	0	
Neil Sullivan	1	1	
Scott Parker	1	0	
Glen Johnson	1	0	
Sorele Fotso Ndjitap Geremi	1	0	
Alexis Nicolas	1	0	
Marcel Desailly	1	0	
Robert Huth	0	1	
Filipe de Oliveira	0	1	
Damien Duff	0	1	
Emmanuel Petit	0	1	

Champions League

Player	Apps	Subs	Goals
Frank Lampard	13	1	4
John Terry	13	0	
Wayne Bridge	11	2	2
William Gallas	11	0	1
Carlo Cudicini	11	0	
Claude Makelele	11	0	
Eidur Gudjohnsen	8	2	3
Glen Johnson	8	1	1
Hernan Crespo	7	3	2
Damien Duff	7	4	1
Marcel Desailly	7	1	
Sorele Fotso Ndjitap Geremi	7	3	
Adrian Mutu	6	1	1

Jesper Gronkjaer	6	4	1
Juan Sebastian Veron	5	1	
Jimmy Floyd Hasselbaink	4	4	2
Scott Parker	4	1	
Mario Melchiot	4	1	
Celestine Babayaro	3	0	
Marco Ambrosio	3	0	
Joe Cole	3	5	
Emmanuel Petit	2	0	
Robert Huth	1	1	1
Mikael Forssell	1	0	
Mario Stanic	1	0	
Carlton Cole	0	1	

Carling Cup

Player	Apps	Subs	Goals
Jimmy Floyd Hasselbaink	3	0	2
Glen Johnson	3	0	
Celestine Babayaro	3	0	
Sorele Fotso Ndjitap Geremi	3	0	
Joe Cole	2	1	2
Jesper Gronkjaer	2	1	
Mario Melchiot	2	0	
Neil Sullivan	2	0	
Damien Duff	2	0	
John Terry	2	0	
Eidur Gudjohnsen	1	0	2
Frank Lampard	1	1	
Marcel Desailly	1	0	
Marco Ambrosio	1	0	
William Gallas	1	0	
Claude Makelele	1	1	
Hernan Crespo	1	1	
Robert Huth	1	0	
Juan Sebastian Veron	1	0	
Mario Stanic	0	2	
Adrian Mutu	0	1	

Chelsea Top Scorers (All Competitions)

Jimmy Floyd Hasselbaink	18
Frank Lampard	15
Eidur Gudjohnsen	13
Hernan Crespo	12
Adrian Mutu	10
Damien Duff	6

CHELSEA TRANSFERS AND LOANS (SINCE ROMAN ABRAMOVICH JOINED CLUB)

Transfers in

15/07/2003	JOHNSON, Glen	West Ham United	£6,000,000
16/07/2003	GEREMI, Sorele Fotso Ndjitap	Real Madrid	£7,000,000
21/07/2003	BRIDGE, Wayne	Southampton	£7,000,000
21/07/2003	DUFF, Damien	Blackburn Rovers	£17,000,000
06/08/2003	COLE, Joe	West Ham United	£6,600,000
07/08/2003	VERON, Juan Sebastian	Manchester United	£12,500,000
14/08/2003	MUTU, Adrian	Parma	£15,800,000
25/08/2003	SMERTIN, Alexei	Bordeaux	£3,450,000
26/08/2003	CRESPO, Hernan	Inter Milan	£16,800,000
29/08/2003	SULLIVAN, Neil	Tottenham Hotspur	Free
31/08/2003	ROCASTLE, Craig	Slough Town	Free
31/08/2003	MAKELELE, Claude	Real Madrid	£16,600,000
30/01/2004	PARKER, Scott	Charlton Athletic	£10,000,000

Transfers out

02/07/2003	ZOLA, Gianfranco	Cagliari	Free
17/07/2003	EVANS, Rhys	Swindon Town	Free
18/07/2003	MORRIS, Jody	Leeds United	Free
21/07/2003	LE SAUX, Graeme	Southampton	Undisclosed fee
23/07/2003	ANIS, Jean-Yves	Partick Thistle	Free
31/07/2003	DE GOEY, Ed	Stoke City	Free
01/08/2003	COUSINS, Scott	Hendon	Free
21/08/2003	KNIGHT, Leon	Brighton and Hove Albion	Undisclosed

Loans

24/07/2003	KNIGHT, Leon	Brighton and Hove Albion	2 month loan
20/08/2003	COLE, Carlton	Charlton Athletic	Loan to end of 2004/05 season
27/08/2003	SMERTIN, Alexei	Portsmouth	

28/08/2003	FORSSELL, Mikael	Birmingham City	Loan to end of 2004/05 season
30/08/2003	ZENDEN, Boudewijn	Middlesbrough	Season loan
16/09/2003	PIDGELEY, Lenny	Watford	
19/09/2003	KITAMIRIKE, Joel	Brentford	Season loan
30/01/2004	KNEISSL, Sebastian	Dundee	Loan to end of season
30/01/2004	KEENAN, Joe	Westerlo	Loan to end of season
31/01/2004	DI CESARE, Valerio	Avellino	Loan to end of season
13/02/2004	ROCASTLE, Craig	Barnsley	
25/03/2004	ROCASTLE, Craig	Lincoln City	

MISCELLANEOUS

During the 2003/04 Champions League campaign Chelsea had 23 different players starting on the bench.

Chelsea picked up 46 yellows and 3 reds during the season, with Robert Huth being the worst offender with 7 yellows and a red.

Statistics provided by Mark Baber of the Association of Football Statisticians, and correct to 30 June 2004.

Photographic acknowledgments

Page 1, (top) © Stringer/Getty Images, (bottom) © Stuart Franklin/Action Images; Page 2, (top) © Steve Morton/Empics, (middle) © Tim Ockenden/PA Photos, (bottom) © Matthew Fearn/PA Photos; Page 3, (top) © Matt Dunham/Corbis, (bottom) © Ben Radford/Getty Images; Page 4, (top and bottom) © Ben Radford/Getty Images; Page 5, (top) © Vincenzo Pinto/Getty Images, (bottom) © Ben Radford/ Getty Images; Page 6, (top left) Adrian Dennis/Getty Images, (top right) © Shaun Botterill/Getty Images, (bottom) © Mike Hewitt/Getty Images; Page 7, (top) © European Press Agency/PA Photos, (middle) © Sean Dempsey/PA Photos, (bottom) © Shaun Botterill/Getty Images; Page 8, (top left) © Rudy Lhome/Action Images, (top right) © Paul Gilham/ Action Images, (bottom left) © Marcello Pozzetti/IPS, (bottom right) © David Lodge/Big Pictures; Page 9, © John Walton/Empics; Page 10, (top) © David Bebber/Corbis, (middle) © Matthew Ashton/Empics, (bottom) © Peter MacDiarmid/Reuters; Page 11, (top) © PA Photos, (middle) © Alex Morton/Action Images, (bottom) © Warren Little/Getty Images; Page 12, (top left and right) © Nick Potts/PA Photos, (bottom left) © Sean Dempsey/PA Photos, (bottom right) © Nick Potts/PA Photos; Page 13, (top) © Robin Hume/Rex Features, (middle) © Nigel French/Empics, (bottom) © Jed Leicester/Corbis; Page 14, © Corbis; Page 15, (top) © Andrew Budd/Action Images, (middle) © Jed Leicester/Corbis, (bottom) © Marcello Pozzetti/IPS; Page 16, (top) © Rex Features, (middle and bottom) © Ben Radford/Getty Images.